LOST MONSTERS

First published in 2009 by Oberon Books Ltd
521 Caledonian Road, London N7 9RH
Tel: 020 7607 3637 / Fax: 020 7607 3629
e-mail: info@oberonbooks.com
www.oberonbooks.com

A catalogue record for this book is available from the British Library.

ISBN: 978-1-84002-929-1

Cover design by Uniform

For Amelia Stephens

Special thanks go to Amelia Stephens, Matt Wilde, Suzanne Bell, Gemma Bodinetz, Deborah Aydon and Lindsay Rodden for their ideas and support. Thank you to all the actors who were involved in the workshops, the development and the production of the play. Mum and Dad for indulging my interest in mini beasts and buying me a microscope complete with slides and phials, containing various creepy crawlies for my ninth birthday. Paul McMullen for inspiration and David Attenborough for the amazing *Life in the Undergrowth*.

Characters

MICKEY

30 – From Liverpool. Tracksuited and as fit as a panther. King of the streets since he was fifteen. Cockroach.

SIAN

16 – From a seaside town. Goth clothes, eight months pregnant, rebelling against her middle class background, chalky fingers. Ladybird.

JONESY

20 – From anywhere in the UK. On the autistic spectrum and a brain full of buttons and bees. Crane fly.

RICHARD

45-50 – From Yorkshire. Eccentric, recluse; as sharp as a bee sting but none of the bumbling. Trapdoor spider.

Man is the unnatural animal, the rebel child of nature, and more and more does he turn himself against the harsh and fitful hand that reared him.

A Modern Utopia H G Wells

Thou wert but a lost monster.

The Tempest Shakespeare

Prologue

Early evening. A storm is building. We can hear a busy motorway. A hooded figure sits watching an open suitcase. Inside the case is a diorama of a valley with an old house in the middle. The valley is surrounded by a road that connects to nothing else. A yellow wind-up toy car is following the road around. It stops. The hooded figure winds it up and sets it off again, as the storm builds and thunder cracks. He suddenly slams the suitcase shut. There is a explosion within the suitcase. It jumps a little, as smoke seeps out of the sides. Then it is swallowed by the ground as the hooded figure disappears.

Act One

SCENE ONE – WASHED ASHORE

A short while later. We can still hear the storm, but the wind has died down, and heavy rain drums hard all around us.

Dim lighting reveals a large study of a big old Edwardian country house, in a valley, surrounded by a motorway. The first thing we notice is the wall on stage right covered in different sized cabinet-like doors of various designs and eras; some of them are out of reach. There is a small couch and a small coffee table next to it, with a top of solid amber; something insect-like seems to lurk within it. Some black and yellow stuffing is coming loose from the couch. There is also a taller dining table which is quite small with one chair tucked under it. An upright piano stands under a bay window upstage right, some of the window panes have been replaced by boards, and there is a door opposite on the right, almost hidden amongst the other smaller doors. There is also a long chain hanging down from a hole in the ceiling, with a hatch next to it. The end of the chain stops about six foot above the floor.

MICKEY enters, breaking into the house by loosening a board and climbing in through the bay window. He has a deep wound in his left arm. His clothes are soaked by the rain and blood. The wound is bleeding heavily. He looks around the room, then exits through the door on the right. A few moments later he returns with a saturated SIAN and JONESY, who he has let in through the back door. They are all out of breath. MICKEY tries the light switch but nothing happens. SIAN is clutching her belly, she is heavily pregnant.

SIAN: What is that smell?

JONESY sits down.

MICKEY: (*To JONESY.*) What are yer doin?

JONESY: Sitting down.

MICKEY drags JONESY over to the window.

MICKEY: Keep an eye on that car.

JONESY: It's alright, we lost them ages ago.

MICKEY: Doesn't matter; car's on top up there.

JONESY goes to the window and looks out.

Make sure yer tell me if anyone pulls up by it. Right?

JONESY: Right.

SIAN: Have you checked upstairs?

MICKEY: I need to rest first.

JONESY: We're too clever for that lot.

MICKEY: Have you lost the plot?

JONESY: We got away Mickey.

MICKEY: Not before they took a big chunk out of me arm.

JONESY: Is it alright?

MICKEY: Is it fuck alright.

JONESY: Let's have a look.

MICKEY: I said keep yer eye on the car.

JONESY: I can only just make it out.

SIAN: Bastards.

MICKEY starts looking around the room. He looks at the hatch-like doors. He tries a few but they won't open. He spots a large church-type candle in a tall, ornate pewter holder. He moves it into a position he's happy with and lights it with his lighter. The room lights up a bit and the shadows flicker, adding to the creepiness of the room.

MICKEY: Yer should get them wet clothes off.

SIAN: I'll be alright.

MICKEY holds his bleeding arm close to the candle flame.

MICKEY: Look at the kip of that.

JONESY: Needs stitches that.

MICKEY: Brought yer sewin kit have yer?

JONESY: I haven't got a sewing kit.

MICKEY: Well I'll have to bleed to death then won't I?

JONESY: Put a tourniquet around it; like in the cowboy films.

MICKEY: Yer what?

JONESY: You need a stick and a long piece of cloth, and you tie it above the cut and every twenty minutes you turn the stick, and it stops you from bleeding to death.

MICKEY: That's enough. (*Beat.*) It's fuckin dead hot in here.

MICKEY takes off his upper clothes, revealing a well toned, muscular body; he has a big scar across his back. SIAN takes off her coat.

SIAN: I need a drink. Me throat's like sandpaper.

MICKEY: Get her a drink Jonesy. I seen a kitchen on the way in. (*Beat.*) It fuckin stinks in here.

JONESY: Are you going to bleed to death Mickey?

SIAN: He told you to get me a drink didn't he?

There is a sudden grumbling sound from above, almost like the house itself has a bad case of indigestion. They all look up at the ceiling.

What was that?

MICKEY: Jonesy, check upstairs.

21

JONESY: Okey dokey.

MICKEY: Any trouble, shout and run back down.

SIAN: Get some water, on your way back.

JONESY goes. MICKEY takes up sentry at the window.

MICKEY: How am I gonna stop it from bleedin? Little bastard scraped the bone.

SIAN: You shouldn't have left me on me own.

MICKEY: I was having a burst Sian. What am I supposed to do? Take yer in with me?

SIAN: The little chavs were videoing us.

MICKEY: Did they get me?

SIAN: I don't know; I was on the floor by the time you came wading in. Never mind their phones; CCTV everywhere Mickey. You'll be all over the television by tonight.

MICKEY: (*Negative.*) Great!

SIAN: (*Disgusted.*) You were like some sort of rabid animal. You could hear their bones snapping and there were teeth flying everywhere.

MICKEY: I was protecting you and the baby.

SIAN: Have you ever heard of reasonable force Mickey?

MICKEY: None of this would have happened if I'd stayed solo would it?

SIAN: You're like a broken record you.

MICKEY: Puttin me on top.

SIAN: The one who pulled the knife on you Mickey. It didn't look like he was breathing.

MICKEY: I think I crushed his windpipe.

SIAN: You could have just pushed him over or something.

JONESY enters holding a plastic bottle of water.

JONESY: H_2O.

MICKEY: Where did you get that?

JONESY: There are loads of them in the kitchen.

SIAN: Give it here then.

JONESY hands over the bottle.

MICKEY: What's up there?

JONESY: Don't know; all the doors are locked.

SIAN: I need to clean this.

SIAN pours water over the wound and tries to clean it.

Jonesy get us some more.

JONESY goes to go.

Hang on. Let me rip yer sleeve off.

JONESY: What for?

SIAN: To blow me nose with, what do you think?

JONESY: Erm... I'm cold.

SIAN: It's boiling in here.

JONESY: It's me only shirt.

SIAN: I don't care.

MICKEY: I'll get yer another shirt.

JONESY: When?

MICKEY: Soon as.

JONESY: I like the patterns on it.

SIAN: He needs a bandage Jonesy.

SIAN rips the sleeve off.

MICKEY: Let's have a look at you first.

SIAN: Later.

MICKEY: Yer don't look good.

SIAN: We have to fix you first.

MICKEY: What about the baby?

SIAN: She's fine.

JONESY: You've lost a lot of blood Mickey.

MICKEY: I might lose you in a minute.

JONESY: What have I done?

MICKEY: Was you pickin up litter again?

JONESY: Well…sort of…

SIAN begins bandaging MICKEY with the sleeve.

SIAN: Yes you were.

JONESY: But I was just putting it back.

MICKEY: What have I told yer?

JONESY: (*Mimics MICKEY.*) Yer can't pick anythin up what's been dropped, unless it's worth somethin.

MICKEY: So what was yer doin then?

JONESY: It hadn't been dropped. I was only picking up litter what had blew out the bin.

MICKEY: How the fuck do you know it had blew out the bin?

JONESY: I was watching it.

MICKEY: You was watchin the bin?

JONESY: I like watching bins Mickey. They attract wasps.

MICKEY: If you ever pick up any rubbish again, whether it's blew out of a bin or out of an angel's fuckin arse, I swear to God, I am goin to dump yer. Yer got that?

JONESY: Yes.

MICKEY: I mean haven't yer got no street smarts yet?

JONESY: I just want things to be tidy.

MICKEY: If it had just been you, I could have said it serves yer right.

JONESY: I got hit the worst.

MICKEY: You're not carryin my baby.

JONESY: That's because I'm a boy.

MICKEY looks at SIAN. SIAN rolls her eyes.

SIAN: Jesus Christ.

MICKEY puts his hand on SIAN's belly.

MICKEY: I shouldn't have let yer out of my sight.

MICKEY puts his ear to her belly.

SIAN: Wasn't your fault, anyway I'm fine.

JONESY: Are we in a lot of trouble Mickey? Will yer go to prison?

MICKEY: I will if I get caught.

JONESY: But you saved us.

SIAN: Doesn't matter what he did for us. They're just kids.

MICKEY: We're gettin off as soon as I've had a rest.

JONESY: They won't look for us here.

MICKEY: Says who?

JONESY: It's in the middle of nowhere.

MICKEY: It's in the middle of a fuckin motorway. (*Beat.*) I shouldn't have left the car up there.

SIAN: You were going too fast.

MICKEY: Nah, it felt like somethin hit us. (*Beat.*) It's bound to get spotted.

SIAN: It's not like we could have pushed it.

MICKEY: First thing they'll do when they find it is look down here, and put two and two together, and then what?

JONESY's face contorts. He knows he shouldn't but is compelled to complete the sum.

JONESY: Four.

JONESY gives off an awkward laugh, and takes out a sachet of his sugar and eats it.

SIAN: We just have to keep our heads down until it blows over.

MICKEY: Too right, because they'll have your fingerprints.

SIAN: How will they?

MICKEY: What was yer doin when it all went off?

SIAN: Me pavement art. I'd already got fifteen quid an all; bastards kicked it down the grid.

MICKEY: And what do yer do it with?

SIAN: Chalk.

MICKEY: Yeah, and so yer prints will be all over the pavement. No more drawin for you.

SIAN: It makes us money.

MICKEY: You'll have to think of something else to do.

SIAN: Like what?

MICKEY: I don't know…face paintin.

SIAN: What?

MICKEY: It's art in'it?

SIAN: Don't be so stupid!

MICKEY: I'm not stupid, I'm… Ow!

SIAN: Keep still then.

JONESY: That won't be enough.

SIAN: What won't?

JONESY: That bandage.

SIAN: Says who?

JONESY: You need that tourniquet I was telling you about.

SIAN: Well then Toto, go and find me one.

JONESY: Don't you mean Tonto?

SIAN: That's what I said.

JONESY: No, you said Toto.

SIAN: Toto, Tonto, what's the fuckin difference?

JONESY: Toto's Dorothy Gale's dog. Tonto's the Lone Ranger's best mate.

MICKEY: Keep yer eye on that car dickhead.

SIAN: The blood's still comin through.

JONESY starts to search around.

Jees Louise! (*Feels her stomach.*)

MICKEY: What's up?

SIAN: Your stunt driving shook her around a bit.

MICKEY: Are yer sure that's all it is? They was kickin yer on the floor.

SIAN: I told you I protected her.

MICKEY: That's my girl.

MICKEY touches her hair.

JONESY: Look at the clouds Mickey. Look. Sian, look, look.

SIAN goes over to the window and looks out and MICKEY follows.

SIAN: Have you ever seen anything like that before? It's like they're...like they're dissolving.

MICKEY: At least we can see the car better now.

Taking advantage of MICKEY keeping watch, JONESY wanders over to the other side of the room and touches one of the doors on the wall.

JONESY: Son, termite sting!

MICKEY: What?

JONESY: Most interesting.

MICKEY: What's that then Spock?

JONESY: These doors.

MICKEY: They're locked.

JONESY chooses a door; pulls at the handle and it opens. A horde of pamphlets spill out.

JONESY: (*Very excited.*) Yes!

SIAN: What?

JONESY: Pamphlets.

SIAN pulls a face.

Shit a pomp level.

SIAN: What?

JONESY: I love pamphlets.

SIAN: You would.

JONESY: I used to collect them. I'd get a big pile for me birthday and I kept them under me bed. But then my Dad said they were a fire hazard and he burned them in the garden along with my collections of tickets and sweet wrappers.

MICKEY: How did yer open it?

JONESY picks up several pamphlets and looks at them.

JONESY: Just did. (*Reading.*) How to Survive the Bomb. What is Pigeon Flu? What to do During a Chemical Attack. Symptoms of Radiation Poisoning. Swine Flu – Are You / Prepared?

MICKEY: / Hang on! What was that?

There is a sound of someone mumbling, and entering the house.

JONESY: Someone's comin in.

SIAN: Shit! (*Panicked.*) Is it them?

MICKEY: Hide yerselves.

SIAN: What good's that going to do?

MICKEY: Just fuckin hide, will yer.

SIAN: You said it was empty!

MICKEY: Get behind the curtains.

> *They all hide. RICHARD enters. He notices the blood on the floor.*

RICHARD: What on earth...

> *He pinches his eyes and looks again.*

God, not another bloody fox!

> *RICHARD closes the door, to reveal MICKEY.*

MICKEY: Now then.

RICHARD: Who are you? What are you doing here?

MICKEY: Bleedin to death. What are you doin here?

RICHARD: This is my home.

MICKEY: You live here?

RICHARD: You've got no right coming in here.

MICKEY: Says who?

RICHARD: Get out.

MICKEY: Do what?

RICHARD: Out of my house.

MICKEY: I thought it was derelict.

RICHARD: There is nothing of any value here.

MICKEY: We... I just needed shelter.

RICHARD: Get out!

MICKEY: I'm not here to take nothin.

RICHARD: There's nothing for the likes of you here.

MICKEY: The likes of me?

RICHARD: Come to see what I've got left?

MICKEY: What are yer goin on about?

RICHARD: There is nothing left to take. Even the bees have buzzed off.

MICKEY: I don't want nothin.

RICHARD: So what, you're a tourist? Saw the funny house in the middle of the motorway and pulled over? Thought you'd come down and get a souvenir?

MICKEY: I thought it was empty.

RICHARD: Get out!

MICKEY: Wait…

RICHARD: You're trespassing.

MICKEY: Just listen to me a minute.

RICHARD: I will not be told what to do in my own home! You've had your gawp now bugger off.

MICKEY: Keep it down.

RICHARD: Get out of my house!

MICKEY: If yer don't keep quiet I'm gonna have to shut you up.

RICHARD: (*Seeing pamphlets on the floor.*) What are you doing with my things?

MICKEY: It was an accident.

RICHARD: Are you on drugs?

MICKEY: I don't do drugs.

RICHARD: Of course you don't.

MICKEY: What's that supposed to mean?

RICHARD: Just get out.

MICKEY: I'm losing blood.

MICKEY shows him his arm. RICHARD steps back.

RICHARD: Keep that away from me.

MICKEY: I've lost a lot.

RICHARD: Well go and lose it somewhere else for God's sake.

MICKEY: Look at the state of it.

MICKEY rips off the makeshift bandage; RICHARD backs off.

I haven't got the AIDS if that's what yer thinkin.

RICHARD studies him for a moment. Pause

RICHARD: Very well. Let's get it sorted then.

MICKEY: You what?

RICHARD heads over to his wall-doors.

Are you a doctor?

RICHARD: No. Doctors are overrated, overpaid, pill pushing pillocks. I'm always darning my socks.

MICKEY: I'm not a sock.

RICHARD opens a cupboard; it is also one of the ones that MICKEY was unable to open earlier.

RICHARD: Cross stitch or garter stitch?

MICKEY: You're not touchin me.

RICHARD: Want to live do you?

MICKEY: Yeah.

RICHARD: Well I can't have some hobo bleeding to death in my home. (*Beat.*) This'll do it.

He pulls out a first aid kit and opens it. He takes a pair of surgical gloves out and puts them on.

Your friends can come out now.

MICKEY: I don't know what yer talking about.

RICHARD: I can see their feet.

RICHARD nods to the curtains, where SIAN and JONESY's feet are poking out the bottom. SIAN and JONESY sheepishly come out from behind the curtain and JONESY accidently pulls it down.

JONESY: Oops. (*To RICHARD.*) I like your shirt mister.

RICHARD: I beg your pardon?

JONESY: I like all those triangles on it.

RICHARD: What?

JONESY: They're isosceles triangles.

RICHARD: I hadn't noticed.

JONESY: Isosceles triangles have two sides of equal length. My shirt's ruined look.

MICKEY: Jonesy, shut up.

RICHARD: (*To MICKEY.*) You best sit down.

MICKEY sits in a chair.

SIAN: Do you know what you're doing?

JONESY: Maybe I could get a shirt like yours.

SIAN: Keep quiet Jonesy.

RICHARD hands SIAN a swab and a small bottle of alcohol.

RICHARD: Do you want to play nurse?

SIAN takes it and unscrews the alcohol.

Pass me one of those bottles of water up there.

RICHARD points to a shelf above the door.

JONESY: Right'ho.

JONESY uses a library ladder to reach the bottle and brings it over. JONESY almost falls.

RICHARD: Careful.

JONESY hands him the bottle. RICHARD then offers it to MICKEY.

You need to replace the fluid you've lost.

MICKEY takes the bottle and looks at it with some amount of distrust, as RICHARD takes out a threaded needle.

(*To SIAN.*) He'll dehydrate.

SIAN: Drink it Mickey.

MICKEY drinks.

That's good Mickey.

MICKEY: I'm… I don't… don't feel right.

MICKEY drops the bottle.

JONESY: (*To SIAN.*) I told you, you needed a tourniquet.

MICKEY: (*Panicking.*) Everythins spinnin.

JONESY: Cowboys use them every time.

SIAN: Don't let him die.

JONESY: What a shame we're not all cowboys.

SIAN has poured some alcohol on the swab and starts cleaning MICKEY's wound with it.

MICKEY: Ow!

SIAN: Sorry.

RICHARD: No pain, no gain.

RICHARD pulls out a syringe.

MICKEY: What's that?

RICHARD: A mild anaesthetic to numb the area.

MICKEY: (*Weak.*) No, no anaesthetic.

RICHARD: I don't want you flinching.

MICKEY nods weakly. RICHARD injects him.

JONESY: There are three types of triangles.

SIAN: Shh!

MICKEY: Ow! Fuckin stings that.

RICHARD puts the syringe in his breast pocket and picks up the needle and thread.

RICHARD: This may still hurt a bit.

JONESY: He needs a bit to bite on.

JONESY grabs a door wedge from the floor and puts it toward MICKEY's mouth but MICKEY shakes his head.

You could bite your tongue off.

MICKEY keeps his mouth shut and JONESY lowers the wedge as RICHARD starts to sew the wound shut.

SIAN: (*Cringing.*) God...

JONESY: You've got some brilliant pamphlets Mister.

SIAN: Jonesy!

MICKEY: Me head...

MICKEY starts to lose consciousness. JONESY glances at his watch.

SIAN: He's passing out. Mickey, you have to stay awake.

MICKEY: I can't...

MICKEY collapses in the chair.

JONESY: Fish meat.

RICHARD: What?

JONESY: Mickey looks like fish meat.

They fall quiet as RICHARD continues to sew. JONESY seems to go into a trance, as SIAN holds MICKEY's hand. Then RICHARD finishes. He stands up and pops the needle into his breast pocket.

SIAN: Thanks.

RICHARD: (*To JONESY.*) Sing to him.

RICHARD goes over to the candle, he waves his hand over it, with a quick movement and the flame extinguishes. He then heads for the door.

SIAN: Where are you going?

RICHARD: Stay here. Give him plenty of water. There's something I need to do.

RICHARD leaves. JONSEY sings a verse and chorus of Going to the Zoo, until Sian interrupts

SIAN: Jonesy just…just be quiet a minute.

Pause.

JONESY: Is he going to phone the police?

She ignores him.

I wonder if he'll give me his shirt?

SIAN: This is all your fault.

JONESY: I was just tryin to keep Britain tidy.

SIAN looks away from JONESY and watches MICKEY. She feels a pain and puts her hand on her stomach. She then puts her hand into one of MICKEY's trouser pockets and pulls out a large wad of cash and looks at it for a moment before putting it back. Then she takes some swabs from the first aid box and starts cleaning the blood from the floor. At the same time JONESY heads over to the amber table and admires it. We start to hear the sound of bees swarming around us. JONESY goes over to the back wall and finds a handle sticking out of it, which he pulls; a large case of hexagonal shelves roll out from the wall. On the shelves are many jars of preserving fluid in which float solitary bumble bees and honey bees. The bees in the jars seem to be larger than they should be, perhaps the thickness of the glass has magnified them or perhaps they are monstrosities of nature. There are also various old books about insects, entomology contraptions, and an old Victorian microscope. JONESY is impressed; he picks up a jar containing a bumble bee, and turns it in the light, as the oversized bee inside swishes around in the fluid.

END OF SCENE

SCENE TWO – PICKLED

The living room just over two hours later. The blood has been cleaned up from the floor. SIAN is asleep next to MICKEY. JONESY is looking at the bottles of bees, turning them in the light near the window. MICKEY wakes up. He checks his pocket for the cash and satisfies himself that it's still there.

JONESY notices MICKEY has woken.

JONESY: Hi Mickey.

MICKEY: What are yer doin?

JONESY: Nibs Grove.

MICKEY: You what?

JONESY: Observing.

MICKEY: Yer supposed to be observin the car.

> *MICKEY goes over to the window and looks out.*

> Shit! It's gone.

> *JONESY looks guilty and tries to hide it by putting a hand over his face.*

> How long's it been gone?

> *JONESY squirms.*

> I told yer to keep an eye on it.

JONESY: I got lookin at these bees.

MICKEY: This is bad Jonesy. How long have I been out?

> *JONESY looks at his Power Rangers watch.*

JONESY: Seven thousand, two hundred and thirty-three seconds.

MICKEY: Hours and minutes.

JONESY: Two hours and five minutes and thirty-three seconds.

MICKEY: You should've woke me up.

JONESY: Sian said not to.

MICKEY: How long's she been asleep?

JONESY: Dunno. Too busy lookin at these.

MICKEY: Sian! (*Beat.*) Sian!

MICKEY shakes her.

SIAN: Uh...

MICKEY: Wake up.

SIAN: What...?

MICKEY: Car's gone.

SIAN: Go away...

MICKEY: Wake up.

SIAN: Get off...

MICKEY: What's up with yer?

SIAN: Tired...

JONESY shoves a jar in MICKEY's face.

JONESY: Bees Mickey!

MICKEY: Get that out me face.

JONESY: There are one hundred and forty-three of them here.

MICKEY: I don't get it.

JONESY: I like bees Mickey.

MICKEY: Why haven't they come here?

JONESY: Bzzzz! (*He shoves the bee jar back in MICKEY's face. MICKEY pushes it away again.*)

MICKEY: I mean, they've got the car.

JONESY: This one's Bombus Lapidarius.

MICKEY: Sian!

JONESY: Bombus Lapidarius is its Latin name.

MICKEY: Maybe they're watchin the house from the trees.

JONESY: Seventy-nine bumble bees, and sixty-four honey bees.

MICKEY: We're fuckin trapped if they are.

JONESY: I've filed them all in my computer brain Mickey.

MICKEY: What are they waitin for?

MICKEY checks the window again then runs out of the room. We hear him running around the house as JONESY continues.

JONESY: (*Shouting.*) I'll start with the bumble bees.(*Getting faster and faster as he goes.*) There's Bombus Lapidarius, Bombus Mendacibombus, Bombus Bombias, Bombus Confusibombus, Bombus Mucidobombus, Bombus Eversmannibombus, Bombus Psithyrus, Bombus Laesobombus, Bombus Orientalibombus, Bombus Tricornibombus, Bombus Thoracobombus, Bombus Fervidobombus, Bombus Exilobombus, Bombus...

MICKEY runs back in.

MICKEY: I can't see no one around. (*Beat.*) Where's the feller?

JONESY: He went out.

MICKEY: Where?

JONESY: I don't know. Will you sing me a nursery rhyme Mickey?

MICKEY: Behave. Sooner we're out of here the better. Sian!

SIAN merely grunts. MICKEY starts trying the wall-doors again. None of them will open for him.

JONESY: I like it here.

MICKEY: It stinks.

MICKEY starts barricading the door using the heavy amber table and anything else he can find.

JONESY: I've switched that off.

MICKEY: Switched what off?

JONESY: The smell. I pressed a button. The one that turns off me nose. It's a big silver hexagonal one. My brain's full of buttons Mickey.

MICKEY: I know it is and one of these days yer goin to press the wrong one and your head'll pop like a balloon full of shit.

JONESY puts his hands to his head as though holding it together. MICKEY notices a bottle of water that has been left for him and drinks it hurriedly. JONESY goes back to the jars of bees and picks one up.

JONESY: I'd like to be a bumble bee.

MICKEY: Good for you.

MICKEY paces the room, every now and then he looks through the window.

JONESY: They're very organised. The world would be a better place if we were all bees. It'd be just perfect. They'd never leave litter in the streets Mickey.

MICKEY: No, they just sting yer on the arse, when yer tryin to pick some girl's locks on a nice summer's day.

JONESY: I wouldn't know about that.

MICKEY: No.

JONESY: Bees evolved from wasps.

MICKEY: Me head's like glue.

JONESY: Wasps are amongst the most ferocious and lethal carnivores in the mini-beast world Mickey. There's this one wasp that lands on the back of a large Plesiometa spider sitting in her web and lays an egg.

MICKEY: I need to think.

JONESY: When the young maggot hatches it manages to stay on her back, riding piggy back, absorbing nutrients from her body as she goes about her business.

MICKEY looks through the window again.

MICKEY: Where are they?

JONESY: The night before the larva pupates, Plesiometa dismantles her web, as nearly all spiders do, and eats the silk strands so that she may reprocess it. And then, at midnight the spider starts to spin a new web but it's not the usual orb web but something much more like a hammock.

MICKEY: I wonder if he's got binoculars or somethin?

MICKEY stops and thinks.

(*To self.*) Come on lad think.

JONESY: This new construction will be both her deathbed and a cradle. As soon as she has finished it, she hangs under it motionless and never moves again. The wasp's larva has injected her with a chemical that first of all changed her web spinning habits and now kills her.

MICKEY picks up the microscope.

MICKEY: Injected?

JONESY: The wasp larva then slowly sucks out every drop of nutriment from Plesiometa's fat body, using the spider's long legs like drinking straws.

MICKEY: (*Drawn in.*) Why does the spider make its web into a hammock?

JONESY: Because the wasp grub doesn't want to fall to the ground and get eaten by scavengers. At dawn the grub builds a cocoon, which hangs on what was the spider's death bed but is now the grub's cradle, until it mutates into an adult wasp.

MICKEY: The baby wasp makes it do that with just one sting?

JONESY: Yep.

MICKEY: That's fucked up.

MICKEY looks at the point on his arm where RICHARD injected him, and rubs at it.

JONESY: Wasps were genetically engineering other creatures and plants a long time before humans ever even thought it up.

MICKEY: Better being a wasp than a bee then.

JONESY: You're a bit like a wasp Mickey.

MICKEY: You what?

JONESY: You sort of engineer me to do things I don't want
to do.

MICKEY: What you on about?

JONESY: The fruit machines make me feel sick.

MICKEY: They make us money, which buys you sugar.

JONESY: I thought you borrowed the sugar from Ronald
McDonald Mickey.

MICKEY: Yer should have stopped him goin out.

JONESY: (*Beat.*) I'm hungry.

MICKEY: He'll have gone straight to the busies.

*JONESY puts the jar down and goes over to the wall-doors. He opens
one of them and a pile of tin cans with no labels on them fall out,
crashing onto the floor.*

JONESY: Oops.

MICKEY: How the fuck did you open that?

JONESY: Just did?

*MICKEY looks puzzled. JONESY starts putting the cans back in the
space behind the door. He is clumsy and finds it difficult.*

MICKEY: They should have made a move by now.

MICKEY goes back to SIAN and starts shaking her gently.

Sian yer goin to have to wake up.

SIAN: No…

MICKEY: Wake up!

SIAN wakes up.

SIAN: What's goin on?

MICKEY: I need yer to get yer head together.

SIAN: Christ!

MICKEY: We're in shit.

SIAN: What's new?

MICKEY: I think we're surrounded.

SIAN: We can't be.

SIAN gets up stiffly and goes to the window.

MICKEY: Car's been moved.

SIAN: Why haven't they raided us then?

MICKEY: I don't know.

SIAN: Maybe it's just been towed away.

MICKEY: It's a stolen car.

JONESY notices the chain dangling from the ceiling and stops his stacking and goes over to it.

How are yer feelin?

SIAN: Like shit. What about you?

MICKEY: Like shit.

SIAN: Bingo.

JONESY: (*Sings.*) B.I.N.G.O. B.I.N.G.O. B.I.N.G.O. And Bingo was his name-oh!

JONESY pokes the chain.

B.I.N G.O. B.I.N.G.O B.I.N /

JONESY pulls the chain. The hatchway in the ceiling suddenly swings open and what at first seems like a man drops down, hanging from a cable. It is an all-in-one, Nuclear, Biological, Chemical protection suit, complete with hood and goggled breathing mask. They all jump. MICKEY pulls his knife out and throws it at it; it hits the suit and falls to the floor, with a clang. Then they all realize it is merely a suit.

SIAN: Jesus Christ!

MICKEY and SIAN start to laugh and JONESY joins in but he doesn't get the joke.

MICKEY: What have I told yer about touchin things?

JONESY: Sorry.

MICKEY picks up his knife and looks at the suit.

SIAN: What is it?

MICKEY: Fuck knows.

There is the sound of a car pulling up outside.

Shit! This is it.

SIAN: What are we going to do?

MICKEY: They're not taking us without a fight.

SIAN: They might be armed.

MICKEY: I'll try and steal one of their cars.

SIAN: It's too dangerous.

MICKEY: Just be ready.

A car door slams.

Make sure you do whatever I tell yers.

Footsteps.

SIAN: Mickey…

MICKEY: Sounds like a SWAT team.

SIAN: It doesn't.

MICKEY: They're gonna gas us!

SIAN: I think it's the man.

MICKEY: Cover yer faces.

MICKEY grabs his blood stained t-shirt and holds it over his mouth. The other two remain motionless, staring at the door.

There is a rattling at the door as someone tries to enter from outside. MICKEY waits with the knife, ushering the others to hide.

RICHARD: (*From behind the door.*) What the bloody hell's going on here?

MICKEY looks puzzled.

What have you done to my door?

MICKEY doesn't know what to do.

Open up.

MICKEY: Who are you with?

RICHARD: Goldilocks and the Three Bears.

MICKEY: Yer think I'm gonna trust you?

RICHARD: Let me in.

MICKEY: It's a trick.

RICHARD: Sian, open the door.

MICKEY: Shut up.

SIAN: He's just one harmless old man Mickey.

RICHARD: Sian.

SIAN: Let him in Jonesy.

MICKEY: You stay put.

SIAN: Let him in.

MICKEY: Stay put.

JONESY is torn between commands. Then RICHARD opens the door toward himself, pushes the table to one side and walks into the room.

MICKEY stares at RICHARD in disbelief, because the door shouldn't have been able to open that way.

RICHARD has a big basket full of bits of newspapers and magazines, with a stone on top keeping them in place.

RICHARD: What's going on here?

He puts the basket down on the table.

MICKEY: Where's the police?

RICHARD: Police?

MICKEY: Why haven't yer phoned them?

RICHARD: (*Snaps fingers.*) I knew there was something.

RICHARD puts a hand in his inside pocket and pulls out an old brown Bakelite telephone receiver complete with severed, dangling spiral cord. He puts it to his ear and mouth.

Hello, is that the police?

MICKEY and SIAN look at each other in bemusement.

I've got a trio of tinkering tykes in my home.

JONESY: I don't think your phone works mister.

RICHARD: Quiet please. When can you come and remove them? (*Pause.*) Oh and how long will that take? (*Pause.*) Never mind, I'll deal with them myself.

RICHARD puts the phone back in his pocket.

Paperwork.

SIAN: Why didn't you go and get them then?

RICHARD: Do you want me to?

SIAN: No.

RICHARD: Lucky for you then.

SIAN: I've cleaned up the blood.

RICHARD: Good.

JONESY: (*Pointing at RICHARD.*) Him be a pooh.

RICHARD: I beg your pardon?

JONESY: Hemophobia.

RICHARD: It's not blood I fear but what it may carry. I thought it was another fox.

SIAN: Fox?

45

RICHARD: They sometimes manage to crawl here from the motorway after they've been hit. I call them motorway snacks.

JONESY: (*Pointing at RICHARD.*) Stow a scary monk!

RICHARD: What?

JONESY: Motorway snacks.

SIAN: Good job we bumped into you. I mean what you did for Mickey was really brave.

MICKEY: Yeah.

JONESY: I don't suppose you'd like to give me your shirt mister?

RICHARD: What I'd like, is you lot out of here. Your car's outside.

MICKEY: How can it be?

RICHARD: The sooner you're out of my house the better.

MICKEY: The engine blew up.

RICHARD: Seems fine to me.

MICKEY: It went on fire.

RICHARD: It has a few dents and the paintwork is a bit fuzzed but she's running smooth enough.

MICKEY: But I'm tellin yer it was a write-off.

RICHARD: Look, it's outside, it's working, so get in it and go.

MICKEY: But I've got the keys.

RICHARD fishes in another pocket and then dangles a set of car keys. MICKEY puts a hand to his own pocket.

MICKEY: How did yer get them?

RICHARD: What is this? A quiz?

RICHARD throws the keys to MICKEY.

JONESY: It can't be; there are no scoreboards or buzzers.

MICKEY: Did anyone see yer?

RICHARD: What?

MICKEY: When you got to the car?

RICHARD: It is a motorway.

RICHARD takes the stone off the papers.

MICKEY: Anythin suspicious?

MICKEY looks out the window.

RICHARD: The only people around are you lot, so if you don't mind…

MICKEY: Sorted. Sian get yer arse in gear we're off. Jonesy?

JONESY: I'm hungry.

MICKEY: Nothin I can do about that is there. Eat yer sugar.

JONESY: Me belly's rumbling.

MICKEY: What do yer want me to do about it?

JONESY: I like your bees Mister.

RICHARD: What?

JONESY: I like all your bees.

RICHARD looks JONESY up and down.

JONESY: Bombus Brachycephalibombus is my favourite one. It has twenty-five letters altogether. I like letters.

JONESY picks up a bee jar.

RICHARD: Get your grubby little fingers off that.

JONESY puts it back down.

JONESY: Sorry. Can we have somethin to eat?

RICHARD: This isn't a soup kitchen. You break into my house; bleed all over my floor and then you expect me to feed you?

MICKEY: No we don't. Come on we're goin.

JONESY: But I'm starvin Mickey.

MICKEY: Move it.

JONESY heads for the door.

RICHARD: (*Slaps his side and shouts.*) That's right just walk away.

MICKEY: What?

RICHARD: Leave me here all on my own.

MICKEY: But you told us to go.

JONESY stops.

RICHARD: Yes but aren't you forgetting something?

MICKEY shows his puzzlement.

You owe me.

MICKEY: What are yer on about?

RICHARD: I sewed your wound.

MICKEY looks at the stitches and then back at RICHARD.

RICHARD: I take it you've all noticed the bad smell?

SIAN: Yeah. What is it?

RICHARD: Rats.

SIAN: Rats?

RICHARD: Beneath the floorboards.

SIAN: Lovely.

RICHARD: They're mostly carcases at the moment. I poisoned them. This is their idea of revenge. God knows how many there are but judging by the stench, there's quite a morgue down there.

SIAN: That's horrible.

RICHARD: I'm not too happy about it either.

MICKEY: Yer should've trapped them.

RICHARD: Well thanks for the handy hint and now if you don't mind, I'd like you to go down there and remove them all.

MICKEY: Me?

RICHARD: And then you can go.

SIAN: You do owe him Mickey.

MICKEY: There'll be all kinds of germs and shit down there. Besides we've got to get / goin.

SIAN: / He'll need somethin to eat first.

RICHARD: Of course. Never employ a man with an empty stomach.

JONESY: Can I have somethin an all?

RICHARD: Yes.

JONESY: Thanks mister.

RICHARD takes a can opener from his pocket and passes it to JONESY.

RICHARD: I see you've already discovered some of my tins.

JONESY: Yes. What's in them?

RICHARD: It's pot luck and er…the can opener's a mental temper.

JONESY: What?

RICHARD: Temperamental.

JONESY laughs as the penny drops and goes over to the cans.

JONESY: What if you don't like what you open?

RICHARD: I'm not fussy. Whatever's in the can I eat it.

SIAN: How come they built a motorway around your house?

MICKEY: Wouldn't sell up eh?

RICHARD: Chance would have been a fine thing.

SIAN: How'd you mean?

RICHARD: It's what everyone thinks. That they wanted to build the damned thing right through my land but I wouldn't sell. They couldn't be more bloody wrong. I'd have bitten their hands off. But no, the land's uneven, one lane would have been much higher than the other, so they just went round me on either side. Cut me off like some sort of biblical leper. (*Chuckles.*)

MICKEY: What's so funny?

RICHARD: They did me a favour. It suits me to be cut off from the chaos out there.

MICKEY: There's no chaos out there. It's as black and white as it gets, you just have to fit in and crack on with it.

JONESY: I can't help wondering why these cans haven't got labels on them?

RICHARD: I get them cheaper that way.

MICKEY: Bit skint are yer?

SIAN: Mickey!

RICHARD: No that's alright. Yes Mickey, I am a bit skint as you so eloquently put it. The death of money is spreading like a plague all over the world and I am one of its many faceless victims.

MICKEY: Is that right.

RICHARD: Yes, because money doesn't matter anymore.

MICKEY: It does where I come from.

RICHARD: Not in England. It's gone the way of the trilobite and the pterosaur. As dead as the Dodo and the Woolly Woolworth. They think they can fix it by bailing out the banks with their neatly wrapped packages but that way leads to greater folly. They should have let them fail. Isn't that what capitalism is all about? Winners and losers. Capitalism without bankruptcy is like Christianity without Hell. They're flogging a dead currency. The pound is sunk.

MICKEY: How do yer work that one out then?

RICHARD: Oh come on Mickey. Surely a man like you can see this nation's been hung out to dry by the bankers and the financiers. And what about the politicians? They went and installed Britannia's arse with a revolving door for any Tom, Dick or Hussein who wants to come and live here and erode what's left of our lost and limping culture. Do you realise that there are spite-filled foreigners walking around out there, with bombs hidden in suitcases that can take out an entire city with one dirty bang? Birds and swine carrying viruses that have mutated and are spreading among the population as we speak; and since they foolishly built that tunnel to France, there are rabid animals pouring into the country like rancid water from a sewer. We're being hit from every angle by catastrophe and calamity and it won't be long before only scattered handfuls of people survive, in places like this.

SIAN: Places like this?

RICHARD: This valley is deep; the motorway cuts it off from the rest of the world and the fumes from its endless flow of traffic sterilize the incoming air of bacteria, viruses and other morbidities.

RICHARD goes over to the wall-doors.

I'm very well prepared to sit it out here.

RICHARD flings open a few doors, revealing that they are also full of tins.

They put sell-by dates on tins but there really is no need. The food in them will last more than a lifetime.

RICHARD moves over to the suit that dropped out of the ceiling.

I see you've discovered my NBC suit.

SIAN: What is it for?

RICHARD: Protection against nuclear, biological and chemical attacks. It is more than enough protection from any poison that will rain down from above.

MICKEY and SIAN look at each other. RICHARD pulls the chain twice and the suit shoots back up into the ceiling.

Let them all laugh at the madman in his bunker but I'll have the last laugh, when they sneeze themselves to death, or choke on poisonous clouds, or burn in the atomic heat of a thousand suns, or drown in the great floods, or starve in the famines, or are driven senile by microwave transmitters, or go into anaphylactic shock, because they have eaten Frankenstein food. And as they die, maybe they'll think to themselves, perhaps mad old Richard wasn't quite as mad as we all thought.

MICKEY: You've got it wrong about one thing. Money still talks.

RICHARD: You mean this?

RICHARD pulls out a big wad of money from his pocket. MICKEY puts his hand in his pocket and realises that the money RICHARD is holding is his.

MICKEY: What the fuck…?

RICHARD pulls a lighter from another pocket, which is also MICKEY's, and holds it to the cash.

RICHARD: I could burn it.

MICKEY: Don't!

RICHARD: Send it to hell that little bit faster.

MICKEY: We've worked hard for that.

RICHARD: I no longer need it. I have every necessity here to survive several lifetimes.

MICKEY: That's our future.

RICHARD: Here, it's yours.

RICHARD hands the money and the lighter to MICKEY. MICKEY snatches it and immediately starts counting it.

If you listen hard enough, you can almost hear its death rattle.

JONESY has been looking at the cans. He touches odd ones; runs his fingers over the grooves looking for answers. Finally settling for...

JONESY: Eenie, meenie, minie, mo, catch a Bombus Eversmannibombus by the toe, if he squeals, let him go, eenie, meenie, minie, mo. This one.

JONESY starts to open the can but the tin opener is past it and he struggles.

RICHARD: Keep going; it'll come off eventually.

JONESY: (*Still struggling.*) Blumin hell!

MICKEY: Put some elbow into it lad.

JONESY: I'm tryin.

MICKEY: He's shit with his hands aren't yer Jonesy? He's got no...er...

RICHARD: Dexterity.

MICKEY gives RICHARD a dirty look.

JONESY: It's comin.

MICKEY: If he ever tried to get a bra off a bird he'd probably tie her tits in a knot.

JONESY: What would I want to get a bra off a bird for Mickey?

MICKEY: Fuck knows. Do yer want me to do it?

JONESY: It's coming.

JONESY struggles on.

MICKEY: How come it's so hot in here?

RICHARD: You think this is hot you want to try a month in the Sonoran Desert, studying paper wasps.

JONESY finally opens the can.

JONESY: Wow!

JONESY shows SIAN.

SIAN: Octopus?

JONESY: I haven't had octopus since the first of September 1999.

RICHARD: Enjoy.

JONESY: Thanks.

RICHARD passes MICKEY a can.

SIAN: Thanks.

MICKEY: Yeah.

MICKEY pulls out his knife.

RICHARD: That for skinning bears is it?

MICKEY: It's just a tool.

MICKEY quickly opens the can.

Fuck me, me favourite.

JONESY: Hot dogs?

MICKEY: Yeah.

RICHARD: You'll have to have them cold.

JONESY: I could always shove them up under me armpit for a bit Mickey and warm them up for you that way. The human body generates a lot of heat.

MICKEY: I like them cold. Pass us a can for Sian.

MICKEY starts eating his hot dogs.

SIAN: I'll have mine later.

RICHARD: I'll get you some tools.

RICHARD exits. MICKEY follows RICHARD to the door, peaking through the crack when he's gone. JONESY gobbles his octopus.

MICKEY: What the fuck's that all about?

SIAN: What?

MICKEY: Agreein that I should go and get them dead rats.

SIAN: You owe him one.

MICKEY: It's delayin us. The car's right outside. Let's just go.

SIAN: You always say that you should honour your debts.

SIAN smiles like a cherub.

MICKEY: It's only a matter of time before we're tracked here.

SIAN: He moved the car.

MICKEY: But not before it was up there for a few hours.

SIAN: So?

MICKEY: So there'll have been people passin who will have seen it.

SIAN: Who takes notice of a broken down car?

MICKEY: You'd be surprised what people notice. There could be a murder investigation goin on out there.

SIAN: Look, if they do come here, we can hide. It's a big house. We could even hide under the floor once it's cleaned out.

MICKEY: What and he'll just go along with that will he?

SIAN: People help people Mickey. The Jews in Europe during the Second World War hid in people's houses. Like Anne Frank. She hid in an attic.

MICKEY: People don't help people Sian. Not anymore. You were on the ground, while a bunch of kids kicked fuck out of yer. A pregnant young girl, and all those shoppers and workers just stood there and watched or looked the other way. So stop being so naïve and grow up.

JONESY: I read about Anne Frank. They gave her up in the end and she died of typhus in a concentration camp.

MICKEY: See? There yer go. Anyway we don't need him. We don't need anyone. We're alright as we are. If it's not broke don't fix it.

SIAN: I need to rest.

MICKEY: Yer can rest in the car.

SIAN: It's not comfortable in a car.

MICKEY: So?

SIAN: Have you got any idea what it's like being pregnant?

MICKEY shrugs.

And while you're driving the wrong way up a dual carriageway, swerving around trucks and mounting pavements in your pathetic attempt to relive your lost youth, what's going to be happening to this baby? *(Beat.)* It's going to be rattling around in here like an egg in a tombola. *(Beat.)* And then what if you crash again?

MICKEY: I didn't crash.

SIAN: We can't risk it

MICKEY: We can't risk stayin here either.

SIAN: I'm too tired to move.

JONESY peers closely at the thing lurking inside the amber table.

JONESY: Look Mickey, this table's got a big spider inside it.

MICKEY: Eat yer octopus.

JONESY: Did you know money spiders sometimes float so high up into the stratosphere that they actually go into outer space?

MICKEY shakes his head.

MICKEY: Keep an eye out.

JONESY goes over to the window.

So what's up with you then?

SIAN: I just need to rest.

MICKEY: Are you ill?

SIAN: No, just tired.

MICKEY puts his hand on SIAN's tummy and then puts his ear to it. He stays like that for a bit, feeling the movement of his child.

JONESY: Mickey.

MICKEY: What?

JONESY: You could get Hantavirus Pulmonary Syndrome.

MICKEY: Get what?

JONESY: (*Reciting from memory.*) Hantavirus pulmonary syndrome, HPS, is a deadly disease transmitted by infected rodents through urine, droppings, or saliva. Humans can contract the disease when they breathe in aerosolized virus.

MICKEY: Fuckin hell!

JONESY: Early symptoms include fatigue, fever and muscle aches, especially in the large muscle groups – thighs, hips, back, and sometimes shoulders. These symptoms are universal. There may also be headaches, dizziness, chi (*JONESY suddenly stops.*)

MICKEY: Chi?

JONESY: The rest of the page was covered in beetroot juice.

MICKEY: Great!

JONESY: It was *The Comprehensive Book of Pests* what I got from a jumble sale on the second of August 1997.

MICKEY: Did it have you in it?

JONESY: What, in the book?

MICKEY: Yeah.

JONESY: No Mickey.

MICKEY: Wasn't very comprehensive then.

JONESY: Am I a pest?

MICKEY: Pestus in the Arsus Jonesyus!

JONESY: Oh?

MICKEY: I take it yer don't want me to go down there after what he's just said.

SIAN: You won't be down long enough to catch anything. (*Beat.*) Maybe we could stay here for a bit.

JONESY: Could we?

MICKEY: What are yer on about?

SIAN: If we play it right, he might let us, long term.

MICKEY: Am I hearin this right?

SIAN: The baby's coming soon.

MICKEY: And?

SIAN: And I can't have it in some back alley Mickey.

MICKEY: I know that.

SIAN: So, maybe I can have it here.

MICKEY: You've got to be jokin.

SIAN: Think about it.

MICKEY: Sian, even if he let us stay, we're on top here.

SIAN: I reckon the opposite.

JONESY: And me.

MICKEY: Do yers now?

SIAN: They'd be here by now if they were going to come.

MICKEY: We don't know that.

SIAN: Course they would.

MICKEY: You're off yer head, as if he'd let us.

SIAN: I want us to try.

MICKEY: We're better off if we keep movin.

SIAN: You just don't want to stop nowhere for more than five seconds.

MICKEY: Have yer forgotten me plan?

SIAN: No but / we can

MICKEY: / We're almost there. (*Beat.*) Besides this feller's crazy.

JONESY: That's what they said about Noah, when God told him to build the Ark.

SIAN: He's harmless enough.

MICKEY: I don't like it here.

SIAN: The smell will go, when you get rid of the rats.

MICKEY: It's not just that. I'm gettin a bad vibe.

SIAN: You and your vibes. Who do you think you are, Doris Stokes?

MICKEY: Who's she?

SIAN: Don't you know anything?

MICKEY: I know what I need to know.

SIAN: God, I can just see their faces now if I brought you home.

MICKEY: Whose faces?

SIAN: (*Mocking.*) Mummy and Daddy.

MICKEY: I'd smash his face in after what he done to you.

SIAN: Is that your answer to everything Mickey?

MICKEY: No. (*Beat.*) There's something wrong about this place.

SIAN: You're not scared are you Mickey?

MICKEY: I'm just sayin it's weird.

SIAN: Oh shut up.

MICKEY: You shut up.

SIAN: You shut up.

MICKEY: Do yer want a tickle?

SIAN: You dare.

JONESY: I do.

MICKEY: Shit.

SIAN: What?

MICKEY: Where's me beach ball?

SIAN: What beach ball?

MICKEY: Me beach ball. Hang on a minute.

MICKEY touches SIAN's big pregnant belly.

MICKEY: Have you eaten my beach ball?

He tickles her.

SIAN: (*Laughing.*) Piss off.

MICKEY: I've had that beach ball since I was a little sprog.

Still tickling.

SIAN: Get off.

JONESY: Tickle me Mickey.

MICKEY: Come here then.

JONESY goes over to MICKEY. MICKEY starts to tickle him. JONESY starts laughing.

SIAN: Get a room.

MICKEY: He can't help it if he's better lookin than you. Can yer mate?

JONESY: (*Laughing.*) No.

MICKEY: I mean I woke up the other night and turned round and seen yer Sian, and I swear to God I nearly made the sign of the cross.

SIAN: Yeah, yeah.

MICKEY: I thought you was a vampire come to suck out me blood.

MICKEY makes the cross with his fingers.

SIAN: Well you've no chance of getting anything else sucked.

MICKEY: Good because if it's anything like yer kissin, it'd be all dog-eared after a few minutes.

SIAN: What are you trying to say?

MICKEY: You're proper rough you.

SIAN: I'm not.

MICKEY: Look at that.

MICKEY pokes his tongue out at SIAN, who inspects it.

SIAN: What?

MICKEY: Teeth marks.

SIAN: That's because you rolled me onto one of me knitting needles.

MICKEY: No it's because you're / a cannibal.

/ There is the sudden sound of a helicopter coming near, which flies straight overhead. MICKEY runs to the window trying to see it. He looks like a cornered animal. It seems to hover over the house and then moves on.

Shit! The double crossing bastard!

SIAN: It's moving away.

MICKEY: No it's landin.

SIAN: Don't be stupid.

MICKEY: He must have called them in.

SIAN: Listen. It's moving on.

MICKEY: It's a trick; they're landing at the other end of the field.

SIAN: It's gone Mickey.

MICKEY: We're trapped.

SIAN: It's okay Mickey.

SIAN takes hold of MICKEY and strokes his face.

Just breathe in and out and listen.

MICKEY does as she says. SIAN continues to stroke him.

It's getting further and further way.

MICKEY calms down.

See? We're safe here Mickey.

Then the door moves and MICKEY pulls his knife out and readies himself by it. RICHARD enters holding a bag of tools. MICKEY almost stabs him, before stopping himself. RICHARD doesn't see this.

RICHARD: It's only me.

RICHARD hands MICKEY the bag of tools.

MICKEY: Is the car undercover?

RICHARD: No.

MICKEY: They'll have seen it.

RICHARD: Who.

MICKEY: That police helicopter.

RICHARD: What makes you think it was a police helicopter?

MICKEY: What else would it be?

RICHARD: Chinook. There's an RAF base about five miles away. They're always flying over.

MICKEY: Did you see it?

RICHARD: No but the sound is unmistakable; two rotor blades.

SIAN: So we're alright then Mickey.

MICKEY is unsure.

We're alright Mickey.

MICKEY: For now.

Nobody moves for a moment and then RICHARD grabs his basket and puts it on the table and sits down.

RICHARD: Can you believe some so-called serious types want to go round hugging those bastard kids who beat up pregnant women?

MICKEY: Have you been listenin?

RICHARD: I don't have to listen Mickey. It's all here in the newspapers.

RICHARD holds up a fragment of newspaper.

I'd say anyone who gave them a taste of their own medicine should be handed a medal.

JONESY: Will you get a medal Mickey?

MICKEY: Button it.

RICHARD starts removing the paper from the basket and onto the table.

SIAN: If anyone comes here, will you tell them we're here?

MICKEY: Course he will.

RICHARD: What makes you say that?

MICKEY: Oh come on.

RICHARD: I have no love for the law.

SIAN: See.

MICKEY: We can't trust him.

RICHARD spreads out some of the odd pages of paper and magazines. They are fragments of different publications. He pulls out some sticky tape from his pocket and pulls out a strip, before biting it off with his teeth.

RICHARD: Sounds to me like the little louts had it coming.

MICKEY looks a little surprised, and eyes RICHARD as he uses the tape to stick two fragments of paper together.

Kids out there are becoming a separate species; throwbacks to some earlier form of man. They don't have language; they merely grunt at each other and will slice you open and jump on your head, for the simple crime of not being them.

MICKEY: Where do you get all this bullshit from?

RICHARD points to the papers he has stuck together.

RICHARD: Out there they have the World Wide Web but here I have a web of my own.

JONESY: Wow.

RICHARD goes over to a wall-door and opens it.

RICHARD: Bits of newspapers and magazines blow down here from the passing cars, and get caught in the brambles and bracken; I collect them every day and piece them together.

He pulls out a thick tome of stuck-together newspaper and magazine fragments and flicks through their crinkly pages, reading out headlines as he goes.

Burglaries and Muggings Up As Recession Bites. Knives Ban Fails. Amazing MI5 Security Leak Leaves Us Open to Terror. Al-Qaeda Target the Premiership. Nuclear War and Environmental Disaster Looming As American Influence Wanes, Warns Terrifying New US Report. Pig Flu Pandemic – Britain Orders Thirty-two Million Masks. Jellyfish on the Menu as Edible Fish Stocks Become Extinct. One-third of All Coral Reef Species Face Extinction. Global Warming Puts the Arctic on Thin Ice. New Global Warming Threat as Scientists Discover Massive Methane 'Time Bomb' Under the Arctic Seabed. Swine Flu May Strike Forty Percent of Britons. Randy Wife Breaks Her Noisy Sex Ban.

SIAN: Don't you think it's all a bit one-sided?

RICHARD: It's all here. (*Taps the tome.*)

SIAN: And you believe it?

RICHARD: All this is litter to the people who toss it out of their cars but to me they are the final fragments of man's last hurrah.

JONESY: I like picking up litter as well but I put it in the bin.

RICHARD: Good for you.

JONESY: Mickey, if I stuck it all together in books like him, would I be able to pick up litter then?

MICKEY: Floorboards.

MICKEY takes a claw hammer from the bag RICHARD gave him.

Any spot in particular like er...?

RICHARD: Richard.

MICKEY: Richard.

RICHARD: Not really.

MICKEY chooses a spot.

You better eat something more, and drink this, you'll be very dehydrated; you lost a lot of blood. Need to keep your fluids up.

RICHARD takes an unlabelled bottle of water from his pocket and hands it to MICKEY. There is tension between them. MICKEY knocks it back, he then goes over to the cans and takes one and opens it with his knife; it's tomato soup. He starts drinking it out of the can, and it spills down his chin.

SIAN: God, Mickey, you've got the manners of a troll.

JONESY: (*To RICHARD.*) Stroll a neon farm.

MICKEY: I don't need no label to know that this is Heinz.

JONESY: How Mickey?

MICKEY: Heinz is Cream of Tomato Soup. Them cheap ones are more like Ghost of Tomato Soup.

MICKEY knocks it all back.

Very nice.

SIAN: I didn't think Neanderthals had taste.

MICKEY starts prizing up the floorboards to make a hole he can get through.

RICHARD: He'll need a bag.

RICHARD heads for the kitchen.

MICKEY: Soon as I've done this we're gone. Make sure yers keep an eye out and don't trust him.

SIAN: He's nice.

MICKEY: Oh yeah, he's lovely.

The boards are coming up easily. The house suddenly groans. They all look at the ceiling and then the hole MICKEY has made.

I can't fuckin wait to get out of here.

RICHARD comes back in with a bin liner and puts it down next to MICKEY.

RICHARD: For the rats.

MICKEY: These boards are rotten by the way.

MICKEY prises the last board up.

Right that's them up. Do yer mind if I wear that er... NBC suit? Just in case there's any germs like.

RICHARD: No it's mine. You might damage it. It'll be no good to me then.

MICKEY: I'll be careful.

RICHARD: I've an old bee keeping outfit in the shed.

MICKEY: (*Exasperated.*) Nice one. That'll have to do then won't it?

RICHARD: It's quite cumbersome.

MICKEY: Never mind that, I don't want to catch that er...

JONESY: My saliva run a dry snore thump.

MICKEY: That's the one, hantivirus thingio.

RICHARD: You'll find the shed just outside, it's in...

There is the sudden sound of sirens, getting nearer. MICKEY jumps up and closes on RICHARD.

MICKEY: Bastard! You was just stallin us 'til they got here.

RICHARD: Don't be absurd.

MICKEY: I'll kill yer!

MICKEY moves toward RICHARD.

SIAN: Mickey!

RICHARD: It's a motorway Mickey. Probably a crash. If so it'll be the third one this week.

MICKEY: They're comin here!

SIAN: No, listen!

The sirens are getting further away again.

MICKEY: We should've kept movin.

SIAN: They've passed us.

MICKEY: They want me bad.

RICHARD: They're either chasing some speeder or heading for a crash point further up.

MICKEY: They're sneaky; they'll try any trick to catch me out.

SIAN: He's right Mickey.

RICHARD: Listen for God's sake.

MICKEY stares at RICHARD.

MICKEY: I don't understand. I don't…

RICHARD: Just take a few deep breaths.

MICKEY: You what?

RICHARD: It'll help you relax.

MICKEY glares at RICHARD and then takes some deep breaths.

JONESY: Mickey's a hod heat.

RICHARD smiles at JONESY and nods.

SIAN: Mickey.

MICKEY: What?

SIAN: The rats.

MICKEY waits a minute and slowly accepts the danger has passed and then heads for the door.

RICHARD: The shed's open. You'll find the outfit in a blue suitcase in the right hand corner.

MICKEY leaves. SIAN takes out a pair of knitting needles and half-made baby sized cardigan from her bag.

JONESY: Oh My boar hips succumb babble.

RICHARD: Pardon?

JONESY: Bombus Brachycephalibombus. There are loads more you can do. Like: Bribable hob shop may succumb. (*Beat.*) I've memorised all seventy-nine of your bumble bees' Latin names mister.

RICHARD: I doubt that.

SIAN starts to knit.

JONESY: (*Rattling them out.*) Bombus hortorum, Bombus ruderatus, Bombus cullumanus, Bombus subterraneus, Bombus distinguendus, Bombus sylvarum, Bombus terrestris, Bombus affinis, Bombus bimaculatus, Bombus borealis, Bombus griseocollis, Bombus fervidus, Bombus flavifrons, Bombus fridgidus, bombus…

SIAN: Alright Jonesy, I'll make you eat them if you say any more.

RICHARD: That's absolutely amazing.

JONESY: Do you want me to carry on?

SIAN: No!

RICHARD: I'm very impressed.

JONESY: I've catalogued them in the filing cabinet in the bee section. (*Taps his skull.*) I've got a computer brain.

RICHARD: You certainly have a good memory. That's quite… Well I mean…that's quite something.

JONESY: I don't ever really forget nothin, except for silly things, like tying my shoelaces or pulling me fly up.

RICHARD: (*To SIAN.*) Eidetic memory.

JONESY: I made a whole bus stop full of girls scream once because I'd left me fly open, and me willy poked out.

SIAN: Don't remind us. We had to scarper from that town an all.

RICHARD: You keep movin from town to town?

JONESY: On the fruit machine trail. Are you an entomologist?

RICHARD: I was.

SIAN: What's an entomologist, when they're at home?

RICHARD: They're not very often home. Usually poking around in a termite mound somewhere.

JONESY: They study insects.

SIAN: Oh, I draw spiders sometimes.

JONESY: Spiders aren't insects. Spiders are arachnids. People who study spiders are called arachnologists.

RICHARD: He's right.

SIAN: They used to call me the Black Widow at school.

RICHARD: I once knew an arachnologist who specialised in black widows. Total idiot. He wanted to find out if humans became tolerant to black widow bites after being bitten.

SIAN: What for?

RICHARD: Well you see many animals that graze in long grass that are known to contain a high population of black widows are immune to their bites. So this fellow wanted to know if they'd built up immunity, by being bitten. So he allowed himself to be bitten and went through days of absolute agony. Vomiting, extreme muscle cramps, tautening of the skin, the whole nasty lot.

JONESY: Did it work?

RICHARD: He didn't find out. The whole experience was so painful he couldn't bear to go through with being bitten again.

SIAN: So the whole experiment was for nothing?

RICHARD: Well unlike we entomologists, arachnologists tend to be a bit unbalanced. The world would be a better place without arachnologists.

The light suddenly goes off and, as the daylight has recently moved into twilight, it is quite dark; however the light beyond the door is on. A long shadow of a bulky-looking figure suddenly thrusts through the doorway; it grows as the owner of the shadow approaches the door. A man in a bulky, hooded suit stands in the doorway, silhouetted by the back light. He looks like a spaceman standing in the doorway of his spaceship, who is about to say – 'Take me to your leader'.

SIAN: Is that you Mickey?

The gloved hand feels for the light switch and flicks it on and MICKEY is revealed in the beekeeping suit, he is heavy breathing.

JONESY: Wow. You look dead good Mickey.

SIAN: It's not Mickey it's Dan Dare.

MICKEY: (*Dodgy American accent.*) Dan Dare reporting to Earth Base Alpha One Seven.

SIAN: Dan Dare's British.

MICKEY: (*Dodgy RP.*) I've been met by three strange creatures.

JONESY claps his hands with approval. SIAN giggles. RICHARD looks on, amused.

They're horrible to look at but I may be just as horrible to them.

SIAN: (*Really enjoying it.*) Worse more like.

MICKEY: The female looks like the Bride of Frankenstein.

SIAN: Oi!

MICKEY: And sounds like a foghorn.

SIAN: I don't.

MICKEY: You want me to stuff it and put it in a glass case? (*Beat.*) I don't think we brought enough stuffing.

SIAN: Ay!

They all start laughing.

Come on Dan. Get to work.

MICKEY: Keep an eye out. Here goes nothin.

MICKEY starts to climb down the hole and then stops, halfway.

Hang on?

SIAN: What's the matter now?

MICKEY: It's dead deep, and the fuckin heat.

RICHARD takes over a crate.

RICHARD: I'll lower this down once you're down there. You can stand on it to get back up.

MICKEY: How come it's so deep?

SIAN: Stop moaning.

MICKEY drops down and RICHARD lowers the crate and drops the bag down.

(*Shouts.*) Don't come back up 'till you've got them all out.

JONESY takes out another sachet of sugar and gobbles the contents. SIAN takes up post at the window. She seems frail.

RICHARD: Why do you keep eating sugar?

JONESY: I always have.

RICHARD: It's not good for you.

JONESY: It's good for ants.

RICHARD: You're not an ant.

JONESY: I used to have lots of them in me pants.

RICHARD: Ants in your pants.

JONESY: Yeah.

RICHARD: Did your mother tell you that?

JONESY: Yeah. I like ants. They're a superorganism.

RICHARD: You remind me of me.

JONESY: Do you like ants?

RICHARD: Love them. Ants, bees, wasps, termites. All insects. But I specialised in the social insects. I kept bees outside. People flocked from all over to buy my honey.

JONESY: Do you still keep them?

RICHARD: No. The hives are still out there though, going to rot.

JONESY: I used to have an encyclopaedia on insects. I memorised it all.

RICHARD: The whole book?

JONESY: It's stored in my computer brain. I can see every page. Even where I spilt baked beans on page thirty-two and where I did a big sneeze on one hundred and eleven and caused the paper to go all warpy.

RICHARD: What was on the page you sneezed on?

JONESY: (*Reciting.*) Scientists estimate that ten per cent of the animal biomass of the world is ants, and another ten per centis termites. This means that 'social insects' probably make up an incredible twenty per cent of the total animal biomass of this planet.

RICHARD: (*To SIAN.*) He's quite something isn't he?

SIAN: Quite.

RICHARD: Have another can.

JONESY starts trying to open another can.

SIAN: We're very grateful for all this.

RICHARD: What about you?

SIAN: What about me?

RICHARD: You should have something too.

SIAN: I'm not in the mood.

RICHARD: You need to get your strength up.

SIAN: For when you kick us out?

JONESY is clearly struggling to open the can.

RICHARD: Allow me.

RICHARD takes the can but not the can opener. He twists the top of the can three times and then pulls the top part away as though he has unscrewed it.

SIAN: How did you do that?

RICHARD smiles and hands JONESY the can.

JONESY: (*Excited.*) Alphabet pasta shapes. Yes.

He pours them out onto the table. He then pulls letters out with his fingers very quickly, as though they somehow stand out to him.

JONESY. A. N. T. I. D. I. S...

RICHARD: What on earth are you doing to my table?

JONESY: Oh... Sorry.

He starts scooping them back into the tin.

RICHARD: (*Intrigued.*) No, no, feel free.

JONESY: Thanks.

He starts putting them back on the table again and carries on making a word. They watch him for a few seconds.

SIAN: You shouldn't indulge him.

RICHARD: Why not?

SIAN: Mickey's working on all his bad habits.

RICHARD: There are worse habits than playing with letters.

JONESY: Look, antidisestablishmentarianism.

JONESY has spelled out the word in the sloppy pasta letters.

RICHARD: I wouldn't like to play you at Scrabble.

JONESY: I would. It's my favourite word because it's the longest in the English language.

RICHARD: I know of a longer one. Pneumonoultramicroscopicsilicovolcanoconiosis.

JONESY: Blumming heck!

RICHARD: Forty-five letters compared to antidisestablishmentarianism's twenty-eight. It's the longest word in our language.

JONESY: What does it mean?

RICHARD: A lung disease caused by the inhalation of very fine silica dust.

JONESY: Pneumonoultramicroscopicsilicovolcanoconiosis. That's my new favourite word.

RICHARD chuckles. JONESY starts making the word from the pasta shapes.

SIAN: So do you work for a university or something?

RICHARD: Where are you lot heading to?

JONESY: Blackpool.

RICHARD: You've got family there?

JONESY: Run if a chemist.

RICHARD: (*Thinks.*) Fruit machines?

JONESY: (*Really impressed.*) Blummin eck. You got it.

SIAN: Jonesy has a knack for makin them pay out.

RICHARD: You memorise the patterns.

JONESY: They make me feel sick.

SIAN: You're not the only one. Those places are full of losers. Chewing gum stuck in the carpets and old boiled sweets in every corner. They're so uninspiring. If we didn't need the money, I wouldn't be seen dead in one of those places.

RICHARD: Don't you get caught?

SIAN: They catch onto us after a while, and chase us off. We've been zigzagging across the country from one seaside town to the next heading for Mickey's Mecca.

RICHARD: Blackpool?

SIAN: Then when we've saved up enough money, we're going to Vegas. There are loads of the really big payout machines there.

RICHARD: I see, and you'll have Jonesy to thank for it.

JONESY: My head gets full of reels. Bells, grapes, stars, melons / bars

SIAN: / Come on Jonesy, it's all part of Mickey's masterplan. (*To RICHARD.*) We've been to all kinds of seaside towns, training him up, getting him ready for the mother of all fruit machines at Vegas. We started him on the bingo for a bit and all.

JONESY: (*Sings.*) B.I.N.G.O.

SIAN: He can do up to fifty cards at once. But too many blue rinsed zombies started hitting him over the head with their walking sticks.

JONESY: I've got a scar on me head.

SIAN: And what about the mad bitch who bit your arm and left her teeth in it?

JONESY does an impression of a mad bitch with no teeth.

There's nothing worse than being chased down the street by a bunch of wild grannies.

JONESY: One had roller skates on once.

SIAN: She couldn't half move on them an all.

JONESY: She stabbed Mickey's left buttock with a size seventeen knitting needle.

RICHARD: How did you know what size it was?

SIAN holds up her knitting needle.

SIAN: We kept it as a souvenir.

JONESY: It left a twelve point five millimetre hole in Mickey's bum cheek.

SIAN: That's when Mickey stopped the bingo.

RICHARD: When you've made the big money, then what? You'll settle down?

SIAN: Mickey wants to buy a ranch over there. Somewhere disconnected, where no one will know where he is and we can live off our own produce. Then I can travel out to the cities on my own and exhibit my art there. I'm going to buy an art studio. If I close my eyes I can see it. It'll be a magnet for artists and poets and anyone who gets what it is I'm trying to do. We'll collaborate and get people thinking about stuff they've never thought of before. It'll be a new revolution, through art and sculpture.

RICHARD: What's he running from?

SIAN: We already told you.

RICHARD: No, I mean before today.

SIAN: He had a dog; I think it was the only thing that had ever loved him. It attacked a little girl and Mickey pulled out his knife to stop it but when it came to it, he just couldn't do it. He couldn't kill the one thing he loved and the one thing that loved him. Mickey tried to beat the dog off but I think it was in a frenzy and so the girl was savaged and I think somebody else had to kill the dog but by then it was too late and the little girl died.

RICHARD: So he ran away?

SIAN: What else could he do?

RICHARD: Surely it would have been better to have faced things.

SIAN: Oh come on, what chance would they have given him? They'd have been baying for his blood. No one's going to listen to someone like Mickey. It's been him against the world for as long as he can remember. I don't think anyone ever gave a shit about Mickey... Until me and Jonesy.

RICHARD: Why do people have children, when they have no capacity to care for them? (*To himself.*) It should be one of the ten commandments. Thou shalt love thy children.

Beat.

SIAN: Do you have any children?

RICHARD: No.

SIAN: You didn't marry then?

RICHARD: I was married.

SIAN: What happened to her?

RICHARD: Divorced me and married a blunt object, went by the name of Brian. (*Beat.*) She didn't understand what I was trying to do here. Couldn't see what was happening to the world.

SIAN: That's a shame.

JONESY: I see you've got a piano.

RICHARD: Do you play?

JONESY: No.

RICHARD: (*To SIAN.*) Do you?

SIAN: They tried to force me to learn it.

RICHARD: Your parents?

SIAN: A lesson everyday for months until they finally realised I had the musical talent of a doughnut. Dad was gutted, he'd already told his business partners I could play at concert pianist level. It was a big embarrassment for him when they all came over for dinner and I couldn't even get through chopsticks.

JONESY: Do you know *Flight of the Bumble Bee?*

RICHARD: No, but I once wrote my own piece called *Dance of the Honey Bees.*

JONESY: Wow.

RICHARD goes over to the piano. He stands next to it facing the others and smiles. He then stamps the top once with his fist and the piano suddenly springs to life. The music is fast and busy, and very melodramatic, reminiscent of the musical scores that pianists played against the old silent films.

JONESY starts to dance around the room, lost in the music, his body jerking and spinning. He mimics the honey bee dance, going round in half circles, moving around and repeating the patterns. SIAN finds this amusing. The piano suddenly stops.

SIAN: State of him. Twinkle, twinkle next time please.

RICHARD: My wife hated it when it played, said it reminded her of the motorway. Mind you she hated anything that didn't emanate from Rod Stewart's anus gland.

JONESY: Do you think I'm a good dancer Richard?

RICHARD: Er…very good.

JONESY: Bees dance when they get back to the hive. It's like a language that teaches the other bees where all the best pollen is.

RICHARD: Yes, I've watched that dance close up many times.

JONESY: I went on a talent show, didn't I Sian?

SIAN: He did.

RICHARD: Oh?

SIAN: 'Wigan's Got Talent.' He was brilliant.

JONESY: Was I Sian?

SIAN: You were the best.

JONESY: Then why did I get booed off?

SIAN: I just don't think the people of Wigan were prepared to watch a puppet show depicting the mating ritual of two Leopard Slugs, to the tune of *Für Elise.*

JONESY: When will they be ready?

SIAN: I don't think I can answer that Jonesy.

JONESY: Are you ready Richard?

RICHARD: I'm ready.

SIAN takes two knitted hand puppets from her bag that look like slugs and hands them to JONESY, who puts them on and then, as he hums the tune of Für Elise *by Beethoven, winds the slugs around each other. After a few moments JONESY stops.*

JONESY: Do you think I picked the wrong tune?

RICHARD: Er…

RICHARD suddenly waves his hand in front of JONESY's face and then he puts it to JONESY's left ear, as though he is pulling something out of it, he then reveals an egg-sized piece of amber, with a bee trapped inside.

RICHARD: Look what I found in your ear.

JONESY: I didn't know that was there.

RICHARD: It is Melittosphex Burmensis, a one hundred million year-old bee.

JONESY: Wow!

RICHARD: The oldest species of bee known to man. It is so old that it is still part wasp.

JONESY: Can I touch it?

RICHARD: It's yours. I did find it in your ear after all.

JONESY: Yes, but Mickey says 'finders keepers'.

RICHARD: Well you have it. You deserve it for being such a dedicated entomologist.

JONESY: Am I?

RICHARD: I'd say so. Can you make an anagram from entomologist?

JONESY: (*Face contorts.*) Legion Mottos.

RICHARD: That's quite amazing.

JONESY: I'd like to go on a television quiz show.

RICHARD: You'd be brilliant.

SIAN: The novelty wears off. Give him a number. A big number and don't give him any noughts.

JONESY: Noughts are easy.

RICHARD: Forty-one thousand, eight hundred and nineteen.

SIAN: Times it by itself Jonesy.

JONESY: (*Thinks; face contorts.*) One thousand seven hundred and forty-eight million, eight hundred and twenty-eight thousand, seven hundred and sixty-one.

RICHARD: Wait a minute, how do we know he's right?

JONESY: You can check it on me calculator if you want.

JONESY pulls his calculator out of his pocket; it is smashed.

JONESY: Arrrgh! (*Very frustrated.*) It's broke. Them bad kids have gone and broke it on me Sian.

SIAN: You're lucky it wasn't your head.

JONESY: It's me special calculator.

SIAN: You can get another one.

JONESY: No, this is me special one.

SIAN: No point crying over spilt milk Jonesy.

JONESY: Mickey'll fix it.

SIAN: How's Mickey going to fix that?

JONESY: He will, he will.

RICHARD: I think I might still have one somewhere.

JONESY: I don't want your one, I want this one.

MICKEY, in the bee-keeping suit, suddenly thrusts up out of the hole, and SIAN and JONESY jump with the shock of it.

MICKEY: Blah!!!!

He slams the now full plastic bag down on the floor next to him.

JONESY: You made me jump Mickey.

MICKEY: (*Funny voice.*) I'm not Mickey.

JONESY: Oh?

MICKEY: I'm the creature from under the floor.

MICKEY pulls himself up and onto his feet.

JONESY: Have you seen our friend Mickey?

MICKEY: I ate him up and now I'm going to eat you up. Feet first.

MICKEY closes in on JONESY.

JONESY: That probably wouldn't be a good idea.

MICKEY: Why's that?

JONESY: I've got athlete's foot.

SIAN bursts out laughing. MICKEY pulls the headgear off.

Oh, it's you Mickey.

MICKEY: (*Amused.*) Fuckin hell, Jonesy. Yer one in a million mate.

JONESY: Actually, I'm one in 6.77 billion. I'd have to have been born about fifteen thousand years ago to be one in a million Mickey.

RICHARD laughs; MICKEY scowls at him.

SIAN: How many did you get?

MICKEY: Loads.

JONESY: (*Waving the calculator in MICKEY's face.*) Look Mickey!

MICKEY: The smell down there and the heat; like walkin through a wall of hot shit.

JONESY: It's broken!

MICKEY: I can taste it on me teeth.

JONESY: Those bad kids did it.

MICKEY: (*To RICHARD.*) And you, yer dirty fuckin bastard. How the fuck did yer let it get to this? There's people out there'd kill for a place like this and you treat it like a fuckin shit house.

SIAN: Alright Mickey.

MICKEY: I mean what is it about people like you?

JONESY: Mickey!

RICHARD: I'm not sure what you mean?

MICKEY: Yer go to all this trouble to fuckin survive the end of the world but yer can't be arsed trappin a bunch of rats properly. And why is it so fuckin hot down there?

SIAN: Calm down Mickey.

JONESY: Fix it Mickey!

MICKEY: Yer should have let the rats live, because at least they appreciated this place.

SIAN: Just have a minute Mickey.

RICHARD: No, he's...he's right.

MICKEY: Too right I'm right. I could have caught somethin bad down there, cleanin up his mess!

RICHARD: I'll er... I'll make it up to you.

JONESY: Look Mickey!

MICKEY: What?

JONESY: They broke me special calculator Mickey.

MICKEY: Serves yer right.

JONESY: They broke it Mickey!

MICKEY: Alright, calm down, fuckin hell.

JONESY: Will yer fix it Mickey?

MICKEY: Looks fucked to me mate.

JONESY: Fix it!

MICKEY: It's fucked!

JONESY: Aaaaaarrrrrrgghhh!!!!!!

JONESY suddenly grabs SIAN and starts shaking her.

Make him fix / it.

SIAN: Don't / do that.

MICKEY: / Get off / her!

JONESY: / Tell him to fix it!

MICKEY grabs JONESY and tries to drag him off SIAN and in the scuffle SIAN falls over. SIAN cries out in pain.

MICKEY: Look what you've done now!

JONESY: Yellow car!

JONESY runs out of the room.

MICKEY: Jonesy! Wait! You'll be seen.

MICKEY goes to follow.

SIAN: Mickey, wait!

MICKEY: I'll have to get him back / before he brings…

SIAN: / What about me?

RICHARD: I'll go and get him.

MICKEY: Hang on, wait!

RICHARD goes after JONESY. SIAN twinges in pain and sits, holding her stomach.

Are you OK?

SIAN: No.

MICKEY: What's wrong?

SIAN: I don't feel right.

MICKEY: Did he hurt yer?

SIAN: (*Indicates baby.*) Something feels wrong.

MICKEY: We're getting out of here.

SIAN: No! We've dropped on landing here.

MICKEY: How do yer work that one out?

SIAN: He's lonely.

MICKEY: So?

SIAN: So, if he's gone all soft for Jonesy, he might let us stay.

MICKEY: Not that again.

SIAN: I want Richard to deliver her.

MICKEY: Are you serious? I wouldn't trust him to deliver a message.

SIAN: So what am I supposed to do Mickey? It was bad enough before but now? Who's going to deliver the baby? You? Jonesy? Or are you planning on letting me do it myself in the bottom of a skip, in a back alley somewhere?

MICKEY: I'll figure something out.

SIAN: I've made up my mind. We've come here for a reason. He's goin to deliver our baby. It's fate; it's in the stars.

MICKEY: Stars me arse. I'll do anythin for yers, yer know that but I can't stay here.

SIAN: Can't yer see what this place is? (*Beat.*) An art gallery.

MICKEY: What the fuck are yer on about?

SIAN: I've got these ideas for big sculptures. I could make them here and put them out in the field. I'd have a non-stop audience. Every car or coach or truck that drives past would look down here and see my sculptures.

They'd speak to those people Mickey. Change their stupid closed-up lives. Then they'd be on the news. I'd be famous.

MICKEY starts laughing.

(*Suddenly freaking out.*) What the fuck do you know about art you dumb bastard? The only art you've ever seen is some anatomically impossible cocks drawn on a toilet fucking wall, with your mother's phone number scrawled next to them. I want to stay here and show the fucking world what I'm all about! I have skills Mickey. We don't need Jonesy's fruit machines. I could make us a fortune right here. Provide a proper life for my baby. She'd have everything she could ever want here. You could build her a slide and some swings, and then you could push her while she watched me create my art. Richard and Jonesy could teach her about maths and nature and then one day she'd be ready to go out there and brighten up the world.

MICKEY: Grow up Sian.

SIAN: You're just like them. Mum and Dad and all the rest of them dead end bastards. Putting me down, trying to groom me into something I'm not. I'm an artist and I'm going to change the fucking world, and I'm going to start here, and if you don't like it you can fuck off!

MICKEY: I'm not talking to you when yer like this.

SIAN: All Dad cares about is money and you're the same. 'You can't waste your time with pencil crayons Sian. You need to get into the finance sector like me. Nothing better in life than making yourself a fortune. I didn't pay for a private education so you could waste it away scribbling on pads. Doodles are for dummies!'

MICKEY: Yeah, well he got that right.

SIAN: Maybe he should've beat me a bit more then. Beat the artist right out of me.

MICKEY: That's not what I meant.

85

SIAN: I'm putting sculptures in those fields and it's going to make us rich. You'll be my first study Mickey. I'll call it 'Caveman Without A Clue.' It'll be a big lump of...

SIAN doubles over in pain.

MICKEY: What's up?

SIAN: Go and get Richard.

MICKEY: What can / he do?

SIAN: / Go and get him!

MICKEY rushes out as SIAN puts her hand in her knickers. When she pulls it back out, it's covered in blood.

The lights start to dim toward a blackout, as a baby's heartbeat builds to an almost deafening boom. Then it fades again as we hear a gang of happy slappers taunting and jeering. A dog growls, and then the roar of the motorway rises from the predatory snarl, until it is all we hear.

END OF ACT ONE

Act Two

A few minutes after RICHARD's exit from the last scene, outside in the field surrounding the house, which in turn is surrounded by the motorway. A steady thrum of vehicles can be heard passing in each direction. JONESY is stood holding the bits of his calculator and singing Going to the Zoo. *RICHARD approaches as JONESY continues to sing.*

RICHARD: Are you alright?

JONESY doesn't answer.

Could I have a look at it?

JONESY: What for?

RICHARD: I might be able to fix it.

JONESY: Could you really?

RICHARD: I'll have a go.

JONESY passes the calculator to RICHARD.

JONESY: Can you fix it?

RICHARD: What's your name?

JONESY: Jonesy.

RICHARD: Your first name.

JONESY: Sebastian.

RICHARD: So Sebastian, what happened exactly?

JONESY: Me and Sian got happy slapped. Mickey was in the pub urinating or they would have kept away from me. No one messes with Mickey. He hurt them and then carjacked the car off an old woman with three small warts under her left eye. They'll put Mickey away and then me and Sian will be lost. I can't look after myself.

RICHARD: You just need teaching how to do it.

JONESY: I get into trouble.

RICHARD: I'm not surprised with him hanging around you.

JONESY: I got into even more trouble before I met Mickey.

RICHARD: Really?

JONESY: Yeah and he gets me sugar and finds me places to sleep.

RICHARD: And is that enough?

JONESY: The last seven cars in a row were all black.

RICHARD: They were?

JONESY: That's an interesting pattern of events.

RICHARD: I suppose it is.

JONESY: What's the most cars in a row that have been the same colour?

RICHARD: I don't know.

JONESY: Oh.

Pause.

RICHARD: It's quite strange really.

JONESY: The cars?

RICHARD: You three coming here like this, I mean of all places.

JONESY: We thought it was empty.

RICHARD: But it wasn't.

JONESY: Four silver cars in a row.

RICHARD: I was here.

JONESY: There'd have been five but a red one got in the way.

RICHARD: I've been thinking about the loneliness.

JONESY: It's a bit like a language…

RICHARD: Facing the hard winter ahead on my own.

JONESY: …car language…

RICHARD: Up there.

JONESY: Blue, black, red, black…

RICHARD: Looking down on the flock.

JONESY: …blue, red, brown…

RICHARD: Lost in the drone.

JONESY: …red, green, silver, silver, white.

RICHARD: Watching all those separate lives whizzing by.

JONESY: I'm trying to learn how to read it.

RICHARD: Feeling no connection with any of them.

JONESY: See what they're saying.

RICHARD: Not one companion in that raging river of moulded plastic and steel. How did we become so distant? (*Beat.*) But now you're here.

JONESY: I like it here.

RICHARD: I didn't think I'd ever meet someone else who actually liked it here. My wife didn't. She hated it.

JONESY: We'll have to go soon.

RICHARD: Would you like to stay here?

JONESY: Doesn't matter what I like, because Mickey will move us on. Mickey always moves us on. Mickey has – I fetch yet.

RICHARD: (*Thinks.*) Itchy feet?

JONESY: Wow, you got it again.

RICHARD: It's been a long time since I had any guests.

JONESY: There haven't been two yellow cars or more in a row yet. I wonder why there haven't been two yellow cars in a row? Maybe two or more yellow cars in a row would be a rare letter, like X.

RICHARD absently turns the broken calculator round in his hands.

When you fix me calculator, I'll give you some of me sugar.

RICHARD: You will, will you?

JONESY: What happened to all the bees in the hives?

RICHARD doesn't answer, instead he focuses on the calculator and holding it in one hand he rubs it with the other. This is accompanied by a low vibrating hum, like the beat of a fly that has been slowed down many times. Then he stops and looks at JONESY, who seems distant.

RICHARD: There you are. Good as new.

JONESY: You've fixed it?

RICHARD: It looked worse than it was.

JONESY taps out a calculation to test it.

JONESY: You're the best.

RICHARD: It was nothing.

JONESY: Thanks. My dad was good at fixing things. I'd break them and sometimes he'd fix them, if he could. I didn't mean to break things.

RICHARD: Of course you didn't.

JONESY: Mostly I broke things by accident but sometimes I wanted to see what was inside them. Like the time I got it into my head that Countdown, which was my bestest show ever, was actually inside the TV and I wanted to go in and choose the letters and so I got a hammer from under the sink and broke it open. There was no one inside, no letters, just lots of circuits and stuff. I tried to put it back together but it wouldn't go. My dad couldn't fix it, so he sat on the violet crushed velvet pouf and cried like a baby. I never cry. Apparently I'm incapable.

JONESY puts away the calculator and takes out a sachet of sugar and eats its contents.

RICHARD: That's a very bad habit you've got.

JONESY: Is it? I used to eat sugar from the bowl.

RICHARD: You shouldn't eat so much of it.

JONESY: My brain has to have it or it won't work properly. That's why I couldn't keep still.

RICHARD: You still can't.

JONESY: I was even wrigglier, when I was a kid. I couldn't keep me attention on things, like everyone wanted me to.

RICHARD: I'm not surprised, must have been overloaded with energy.

JONESY: I'd run round the backs of the sofas when everyone was trying to watch telly, and imagine I was a bee doing the bee dance. Why can't people be more like bees?

RICHARD: Because bees are simple creatures, they have none of the sophisticated problems that hinder humanity. We are slaves to the complexity of our hormones, the poisons in our diet, and the chemical imbalances within our overworked brains. Bees created their Utopia long ago but like all great empires they are doomed to time, just as men are.

JONESY: If I ruled the world, I'd invent those pheromones queen bees use to create their highly ordered societies but ones that could work on people.

RICHARD: I'm afraid you've been beaten to it by the processed food giants. They lace their slop with additives that have turned the population into lazy television fodder.

JONESY: I'd like to be a bee.

RICHARD: I'm glad you're not.

JONESY: Bees are all the same. If I was a bee I wouldn't be so different to everybody else.

RICHARD: You just need to find the right outlet for your special abilities.

JONESY: I have special abilities?

RICHARD: Oh yes, but they've obviously been overlooked.

JONESY: I'd make a good bee. I used to be up at four in the morning and buzzing all over the house.

RICHARD: Good Lord! You must have driven your parents round the bend.

JONESY: I can't drive.

RICHARD chuckles.

Nobody could keep up with me. Sometimes me Mum and Dad would cry because of it, because I was so loud all the time. My off switch is hard to find. I don't know why people cry, it's uneconomical.

RICHARD: I don't know about that.

JONESY: Water loss. Some desert tribes don't ever cry, because the water's precious. I read that in a *Reader's Digest*, that also had an article that said synthesised spiders' silk could save the world.

RICHARD: That's because it's so strong. You could make everything from skyscrapers miles high, to / un-tearable clothes.

JONESY: / Un-tearable clothes.

RICHARD chuckles.

My mum collected *Reader's Digest*. She done some other good things an all.

RICHARD: Such as?

JONESY: She sang me lots of nursery rhymes before bed.

RICHARD: That is nice.

JONESY: And she knew where all my ticklish spots were.

RICHARD: She sounds fun.

JONESY: She didn't like me asking her to do sums or anagrams though. Not after a while anyway.

RICHARD: What about brothers and sisters?

JONESY: I wasn't allowed to play with them.

RICHARD: Why?

JONESY: Because of what happened to little Ellie.

RICHARD: What happened?

JONESY: I can't remember. I do remember my Dad shaking me though. He was saying something over and over but I can't remember what.

RICHARD: Where is your family?

JONESY: Oh, they forgot to take me with them.

RICHARD: Take you where?

JONESY: They went on a special car trip.

RICHARD: Didn't they come back?

JONESY: No.

RICHARD: When was this?

JONESY: (*Looking at watch.*) Approximately two hundred and fifty-three million, eight hundred and seven thousand, and two hundred seconds ago, or eight years, seventeen days and eight hours ago.

RICHARD: When you were a little boy.

JONESY: The headmaster sent me home early because I kept hugging Ryan Phillips. Ryan Phillips didn't like being hugged. So I ran home using shortcuts. I made twenty-three scrapbooks full of shortcuts that I invented. I wish I still had them. They was colour coded.

RICHARD: Inventive.

JONESY: Is it?

RICHARD: Very.

JONESY: I got back home and stuffed me face with sugar and went out to the garage to ask me Dad if he knew the square root of one million. Dad liked to lock himself in, I don't know why, they were always locking doors. So I got the spare key from under one of the gnomes, the one with the scarlet tunic, and I unlocked the door. Then this wall of fumes came out at me. It burned my eyes and throat.

RICHARD: Good God…

JONESY: I went inside and there was the car, engine running; it was all glazy with the smoke and heat but I could see them all straight away. Dad in the driving seat, Mum next to him, the baby in the middle strapped in his rainbow coloured seat, Angela on his left and Antony on his right. They all had their seat belts on and they were all white; skin like fish meat. Angela's eyes were open and so were the baby's but they were all funny-looking like glass beads. I felt faint, like the roof of the garage was pressing down on me and it was like I was falling into Angela's eyes. Then Mrs Spencer, our next door neighbour, grabbed me from behind and pulled me out. She took me inside her house and while she phoned an ambulance and the police, I ate her dark brown rock sugar and rocked in her rocking chair, and looked at a painting of a little boy in blue pyjamas on the wall with a tear on his cheek. I was looking at him and thinking – she expects me to have one of those on my cheek. And then I got took to hospital.

RICHARD: Did you have other family? Someone to look after you?

JONESY: They were all busy. (*Pause.*) Richard, why didn't they take me with them?

RICHARD: Er…

JONESY: I can't work it out. (*Pause.*) I think the cars will tell me, if I can learn their language. (*Beat.*) Our car was yellow. And that car Mickey stole was yellow. I think yellow is important.

RICHARD: Did you want to go with them?

JONESY: Well it would have been nice to have been asked.

RICHARD: (*Pause.*) After... After the hospital, what happened then?

JONESY: I had to go and live with a family who didn't have any sugar. They had sweeteners. I don't like sweeteners. They don't fuel my brain. So I ran away.

RICHARD: That's when Mickey found you.

JONESY: Yeah. Mickey protects me and feeds me and gets me sugar. Not just sachets but even this big bag that he keeps for emergencies.

RICHARD: No, look, he's got you traipsing from town to town, walking the streets all day long, and sleeping rough, and then in between that he's got you glued to those fruit machines, lining his pockets on your genius and fulfilling none of your potential.

JONESY: Potential?

RICHARD: I've only known you five minutes but I can tell that you are something quite special Sebastian. You're wasted with Mickey and his way of life. Wasted milking those machines.

JONESY: Am I?

RICHARD: I could teach you things. You could... You could learn how to keep bees, just like I did.

JONESY: Me?

RICHARD: Why not?

JONESY: I'd like that. I'd like that a lot.

RICHARD: I'd like to teach you things. Get you using that incredible computer brain of yours.

JONESY: How?

RICHARD: I don't know... (*Snap.*) You could go on *Mastermind.* Your specialist subject could be entomology.

JONESY: I'd like that.

RICHARD suddenly raises his hands into the air and the sky darkens and the Mastermind *theme music begins to play around them. JONESY looks around him. RICHARD then thrusts his right hand to stage right as though reaching for something and a black leather* Mastermind *chair on wheels flies across the stage toward them, as though RICHARD has summoned it. It crashes into his hand and stops and with his other hand he pushes JONESY into the chair as the* Mastermind *music comes to its climax. RICHARD snaps his fingers and a spotlight encapsulates JONESY in the chair as RICHARD backs off a few paces.*

RICHARD: And your name is?

JONESY: Sebastian Jones.

RICHARD: And your occupation?

JONESY: Milking fruit machines.

RICHARD: And your chosen subject?

JONESY: Entomology.

RICHARD: Entomology. Your two minutes starts now. What name do we give to the outer skeleton of insects?

JONESY: Chitin.

RICHARD: Since the Stone Age, which species of insect is estimated to be responsible for half of the human deaths in history, outside war and accidents?

JONESY: The Anopheles mosquito, which carries the malaria parasite Plasmodium.

RICHARD: Which is the largest order of insects?

JONESY: The beetles.

RICHARD: A queen leafcutter ant mates only once but how many offspring can she then produce during her lifetime?

JONESY: Three hundred million.

RICHARD: How long can a cockroach survive without its head?

JONESY: Nine days.

RICHARD: Which three groups of insects have evolved fungus-based agriculture?

JONESY: Leafcutter ants, termites and ambrosia beetles.

RICHARD: What is the name of an insect's multi-faceted eye, also found in crustaceans?

JONESY: The compound eye.

RICHARD: Which order of insects formed the first super societies?

JONESY: Termites.

RICHARD: How many legs does an insect have?

JONESY: Six.

RICHARD: Why didn't your parents take you with them?

JONESY: What?

RICHARD: I'll repeat the question. Why didn't your parents take you with them?

JONESY: Pass.

RICHARD: Why didn't your parents take you with them?

JONESY: Pass.

RICHARD: Why didn't they take you?

JONESY: I don't know.

RICHARD: Why?

JONESY: I can't remember.

RICHARD: But you remember everything. You have started, so you must finish.

JONESY: I... I...don't...don't...remember

We hear MICKEY shouting.

MICKEY: Jonesy! (*Beat.*) Jonesy!

JONESY stands up and then falls to his knees, his hands scrabbling in his pockets for sugar. RICHARD reaches out for the chair and without actually touching it he flings it back to whence it came. He waves his arms and the spotlight disappears and the sky brightens.

RICHARD: Sebastian? Are you alright?

JONESY: What happened?

RICHARD: You fainted.

JONESY: Oh?

MICKEY's voice from off.

MICKEY: Jonesy!

JONESY: Don't tell Mickey.

MICKEY: Richard.

MICKEY appears.

There yer are. I've been lookin all over the place. I thought you'd been nabbed.

JONESY: I haven't.

MICKEY: What are yers doin?

JONESY: Richard's fixed my calculator.

MICKEY: Have yer?

RICHARD: How's Sian?

MICKEY: She er... She wants... She wants yer to go and see her.

RICHARD: What for?

MICKEY: I don't know; she's in one of her moods.

RICHARD: What can I do for her?

MICKEY: Fuck knows.

RICHARD: Let's get back inside then.

MICKEY: I need to sort out Jonesy first.

JONESY: I'm reading the cars Mickey.

RICHARD: What are you going to do?

MICKEY: He hurt Sian.

RICHARD: He didn't mean to.

MICKEY: I need to make him understand that what he did was wrong.

RICHARD: And how will you do that?

MICKEY: With words.

JONESY: Four black cars.

RICHARD: I'll only go if Sebastian says it's OK.

MICKEY: Sebastian?

RICHARD: Are you OK to stay here with Mickey for a bit Sebastian?

JONESY: Three silver cars.

MICKEY: I won't harm him.

RICHARD: You seem to have a tendency to lose your rag.

MICKEY: Jonesy, have I ever laid a finger on you?

JONESY: Lots of times. Like when you got rid of my nits for instance.

MICKEY: I don't mean like that. Have I ever hit you?

JONESY: No.

MICKEY: So there you go.

RICHARD: I'll be in the house if you need me.

MICKEY: He doesn't need you.

The house suddenly groans; there is something impatient about it. They all look back at the house.

What was that?

RICHARD: I'll go and see Sian then.

MICKEY: We won't be long.

RICHARD heads back towards the house.

You hurt Sian.

JONESY: Richard is going to let me stay here.

MICKEY: Do what?

JONESY: He wants to help me reach my potential.

MICKEY: What potential?

JONESY: He's going to help me get on *Mastermind.*

MICKEY: What's he been fillin yer head with?

JONESY: Richard's going to teach me things and all.

MICKEY: I teach yer things.

JONESY: But you're not clever like him Mickey.

MICKEY: Now hang on!

JONESY: And yer haven't got no house for me to live in neither.

MICKEY: We don't need no house yet.

JONESY: I do. I've decided that I'm going to stay here.

MICKEY: He can't look after yer like I can.

JONESY: I won't need that kind of looking after if I stay here.

MICKEY: Yer don't know what yer talkin about. Alls we've got to do now is get to Blackpool. Just think of all the candyfloss and all those big fat fruit machines waitin for yer to come and light them up.

JONESY: But I don't like doing that Mickey.

MICKEY pulls out his wad of cash and shows JONESY.

MICKEY: Life isn't about what yer like Jonesy. It's about what you need.

JONESY: I'm not sure I need you anymore Mickey.

Pause

MICKEY: Empty yer pockets.

JONESY: What?

MICKEY: You heard. Empty them.

JONESY: But...

MICKEY: That's my sugar you've got and if yer don't need me anymore, yer can give it me back.

JONESY: But then I'll have no sugar Mickey.

MICKEY: Richard can get yer some.

JONESY: He might not. He disapproves.

MICKEY: I said empty your pockets.

JONESY: No.

MICKEY: Do yer want me to empty them for yer?

JONESY: Yellow car!

MICKEY: Answer me!

JONESY: Black car!

MICKEY: Sugar, now!

JONESY: Red car.

MICKEY: Right!

JONESY: Brown car!

> *MICKEY grabs JONESY and forces him to the ground. He then starts to grab the sugar from his pockets and starts ripping them open and pouring them over the grass.*

That's mine!

MICKEY: Yer think you're in control? Yer not in control. You're a fuckin mess. Yer need me to look after yer. Yer think Richard could do what I did? Yer couldn't even wipe yer arse without getting shit on yer fingers 'til yer met me. Remember when I found yer? What was goin to happen to yer if I hadn't stepped in?

JONESY: Don't... I need it.

MICKEY: Oh, yer need it do yer!

JONESY tries to grab the sachets. MICKEY pushes him over and sits on top of his chest.

JONESY: Get off me!

MICKEY takes a half pound bag of sugar from his jacket pocket.

That's my emergency supply.

MICKEY rips it open and pours it over JONESY's face.

I need… need it.

MICKEY: Yer need me.

JONESY: No!

MICKEY: Say it!

JONESY: (*Choking on sugar.*) St…stop!

MICKEY: Tell me yer need me!

Lots of sugar has gone into JONESY's mouth and he has swallowed much of it. JONESY suddenly starts convulsing. MICKEY jumps off him. JONESY stands up, his eyes rolling to the back of his head.

JONESY: Daddy's taking us to the zoo tomorrow… Look me in the eye Sebastian… Don't do that… That's not a proper smile… Look what you've done to the telly… Why are you crying Mummy?… You want to put some calamine lotion on that… He's a psychopath… Is this a sad face or a happy face… She's not breathing Stuart… There were two in the bed and the little one said, Roll over, roll over… Get away from that sugar bowl… Venus's mass is 4.869 times 1024 kilograms… For God's sake, stop repeating yourself… We can stay all day… I'll have a P please Bob… You're too old for nappies… Stay away from him Angela… Is this a surprised face or an angry face… Ooh isn't he clever… If you don't learn to tie your shoelaces today, I'm going to burn all your tickets… I'll shove that calculator down your throat in a minute… Mars has the largest canyon in the solar system… Stop hugging me… Blowflies transmit a wide range of bacteria… Cry you little bastard, cry…

Beetroot... Sorry Sebastian but they are a fire hazard...
Look what you've done... Beetroot... Look me in the
eye... He's unconscious...beetroot...yellow car...talcum
powder...silent night, holy night...beetroot...yellow car...
yellow car...yellow cot...yellow...yellow...yellow...
tssssssssssssss...

MICKEY shakes JONESY.

MICKEY: What's up with yer?

JONESY: There's something missing Mickey!

JONESY leaps up, his eyes wild, body trembling.

I remember everything. My memory is like one big video
tape that I can rewind and watch over and over again from
any bit I want. But there's this one bit that's like the page
in *The Comprehensive Book of Pests* that's covered in beetroot.
I remember going to bed and pulling the blue covers over
me and then waking up in yellow covers and Dad was
shaking me but I can't hear what he's shouting, it's all
beetroot.

MICKEY: What are yer on about?

JONESY: Yellow. The cars Mickey. The yellow cars have the
answer. They can show me what's missing.

MICKEY: They can't.

JONESY: The fruit machines get in the way. Take space. I need
to stay here and watch the cars.

MICKEY: There's nothing you need to know, except what I tell
yer.

JONESY: The cars Mickey!

MICKEY: Fuck the cars!

JONESY: I'll make them tell me!

JONESY suddenly runs towards the road.

MICKEY: Jonesy stop! Jonesy!

BLACKOUT.

The sound of the cars builds up to a loud cacophony. Then there is the screeching of a multitude of brakes, screaming rubber and angry horns. When the horns stop we hear a heartbeat, which gets fainter and fainter, until there is nothing.

END OF SCENE

SCENE TWO – LOST AND FOUND

Following RICHARD's departure from the last scene; SIAN is sat knitting a pair of pink baby boots. RICHARD enters holding a bowl and a knife and fork. He puts them on the table.

RICHARD: Mickey said you wanted me.

SIAN: I think the baby might be coming.

RICHARD: Now?

SIAN: I don't know. Maybe. Soon anyway.

RICHARD: You need to go to hospital then.

SIAN: I want to have it here.

RICHARD: How can you have it here?

SIAN: I want you to deliver it.

RICHARD: I'm no midwife Sian.

SIAN: You sewed up Mickey's cut.

RICHARD: That hardly qualifies me.

SIAN: You've got no choice.

RICHARD: You need to get Mickey to drive you to the hospital.

SIAN: He can't do that.

RICHARD: Of course he can.

SIAN: He's wanted. That boy might even be dead. They'll put him away for years.

RICHARD: That's not your fault.

SIAN: He was protecting me.

104

RICHARD: You'd never have been in that situation in the first place if he hadn't taken advantage of you.

SIAN: Mickey didn't take advantage of me, I took advantage of him.

RICHARD: You're using Mickey?

SIAN: No... I mean I was...that's how it all started but things got complicated. At first I just wanted to escape that sterile bubble Mum and Dad kept me in. I wanted to have an adventure. To see what it was like on the other side...to be lost in the moment. I saw Mickey as a way to achieve that and still be safe. He and Jonesy just appeared in town, hanging around the arcades. I watched them for a few days. I followed them to where they were sleeping under the pier. They had so little and yet they had so much more. They were free and I wanted that but I knew he'd never take me on, so I made up a story. Something that would make him want to take me with him but it was only ever meant to be a means to an end. I'd have my mad adventure and then go back home and take control of my life. But then things changed. (*Beat.*) You know he didn't even try it on with me. Not once. That was all me. I actually think he feared any kind of physical intimacy. But I found a chink in his armour and he was so gentle with me. I think that surprised him. He didn't know what was in him. And then when I told him I was pregnant, it was like a part of him that was dead came back to life. He's given me something I hadn't dreamed of. This baby means everything to me now.

RICHARD: You should go home.

SIAN: I drew a picture once, when we were squatting on a barge. We hadn't been together long. It was abstract. I showed it to Mickey. I asked him what it was. I expected him to say that it looked like someone had thrown up on the paper or something, because that would be very Mickey. But do you know what he said?

RICHARD: No.

SIAN: 'It's your pain.' He was right. I think… I think I fell in love with him then. (*Beat.*) Am I a bad person Richard?

RICHARD: You're human Sian, and humans make mistakes.

SIAN touches RICHARD's face and strokes his cheek.

SIAN: You're a kind man. (*Beat.*) Will you deliver her for me?

RICHARD: Don't ask me to do that.

SIAN: Please. It's the only way.

RICHARD: It goes against everything I believe. This world is no place for babies anymore. I want no part in delivering one.

SIAN: We could stay here. We'd be safe with you.

RICHARD: What kind of existence will it be for a child living here, surrounded by a dead, poisonous world?

SIAN: At least she'd have us. If what you believe is true then I'd rather her stay here than die out there. There's a reason for this baby.

There is a pause as RICHARD thinks.

RICHARD: I'll deliver the child.

SIAN: Thank you so much.

RICHARD: If Mickey will allow it that is.

SIAN: Leave Mickey to me.

RICHARD picks up a can and twists the top three times and somehow unscrews the top off the can.

RICHARD: I want you to eat something.

SIAN: I'm not hungry. Mickey and I chose to be homeless but what right have we got to choose that life for the baby?

RICHARD: It's your favourite.

SIAN: What is?

RICHARD: Peking duck.

SIAN: How do you know?

RICHARD pours the contents into the bowl he placed on the table and, picking up the knife and fork, he takes them over to SIAN.

RICHARD: That would be telling. Eat.

SIAN takes the bowl of food.

SIAN: It's warm.

RICHARD: You'll feel better with it in your belly.

SIAN pokes at the meat with her fork.

SIAN: What are you?

RICHARD: I'm sparsile.

SIAN: What does that mean?

RICHARD: Sparsile is a word that has been dropped from the dictionary. It means a star not included in any constellation and now it is a word not included in any new dictionary.

SIAN: Aren't you lonely here all by yourself?

RICHARD: Better to be alone than suffer the company of / fools.

/ There is the sudden sound of a mass of braking cars on the motorway, followed by blaring horns.

SIAN: Mickey!

RICHARD and SIAN head for the window. The horns are still blaring.

What's happening?

RICHARD: The traffic's stopped.

SIAN: Oh my God!

RICHARD: On the North lane.

SIAN: Can you see them?

RICHARD: No.

SIAN: Have they been hit?

RICHARD: (*Beat.*) Look, it's moving again. No need to worry.

SIAN nods. They stand looking out of the window for a moment.

SIAN: How would you feel about me brightening things up a bit?

RICHARD: If you want.

SIAN: And plant the field with flowers and apple trees.

RICHARD: You should have seen it in its heyday. Flower beds buzzing with bees; the smell of honey hanging in the air. This room was quite special. I did all my studying in here. There was a big electron microscope over there. Cost me a small fortune.

SIAN: Where is it now?

RICHARD: I had an attack of the bailiffs. Nasty little ailment; it leaves you with nothing but your foundations and a few hundred jars of bees.

SIAN: Not much money in jars of dead bees?

RICHARD: So it would seem. They took the butterflies of course. Whole cases of them. Plenty of money in dead butterflies.

SIAN: I could do some good work here.

RICHARD: Work?

SIAN: I could fill your valley with sculptures. That would show them.

RICHARD: Who?

SIAN: My brain-dead parents. (*Beat.*) Just imagine all those people driving past and looking down and seeing all the giant sculptures I'd made. They'd want to get a closer look. They'd wonder who was behind them all. They'd have questions, and some of them would want to stay and add to the collection. Other artists. It could become one of the seventh wonders of the world. Can you see it Richard?

RICHARD doesn't answer.

I feel safe here.

RICHARD: The bees weren't safe.

SIAN: What happened to them?

RICHARD: Wiped out by a combination of a tiny parasitic
mite called Varroa Destructor and too much rain in the
summer. I've seen it happen all over the world. We call it
Colony Collapse Disorder. Before long the honey bee will
be gone and who will pollinate the flowers then? Their
demise will start off a chain reaction of mass extinction
that will finish mankind for good, if he doesn't finish
himself first. I tried everything to save my bees, they
were like my children, everything within my power, but
they died just the same and that is when I realised there
was no hope for civilization. I knew then that if I were to
survive I would have to abandon my life's work and turn
my attentions to survival. The cities will become stinking
tombs, their billboards and signs will be fitting epitaphs for
the human race.

SIAN: Shh. I don't want her to hear you.

RICHARD: How do you know it's a girl?

SIAN: I just do.

*SIAN touches RICHARD's hand. The house grumbles. SIAN looks up
at the ceiling, she looks back at RICHARD, puzzled. He smiles.*

JONESY runs in.

JONESY: Richard!

RICHARD: Sebastian.

JONESY: I just saw, not two but three yellow cars in a row. I
think I'm close to understanding the car patterns.

MICKEY rushes in.

MICKEY: Are you off yer trolley?

JONESY: I saw three yellow cars in a row Mickey.

MICKEY: He only ran into the lanes.

JONESY: They was this close. (*Demonstrates a short distance.*)

MICKEY: I had to go in and drag him out.

SIAN: You didn't!

JONESY: I needed to make them stop.

MICKEY: He nearly caused a major pile up.

JONESY: Get it all fixed in place.

RICHARD: What were you thinking of Sebastian?

JONESY: Three yellow cars in a row.

RICHARD: Promise me you'll never do that again.

JONESY: They spoke to me.

MICKEY: They nearly splattered yer more like.

JONESY: Something's shifted in me brain. It'll take time to process but the yellow cars have revealed / something.

MICKEY: / They're just cars / Jonesy.

RICHARD: / You stupid, stupid boy.

MICKEY: Yer need to get a / grip.

RICHARD: / You could have been / killed.

MICKEY: / It's doin him no good bein here.

RICHARD grabs JONESY and shakes him.

RICHARD: You could have been killed and then what would happen to me? Did you think about that?

MICKEY: Let go of him.

RICHARD: Where would that leave me?

MICKEY: What the fuck are yer doin?

RICHARD: Stupid, silly boy!

JONESY: I won't do it again Richard.

MICKEY pulls RICHARD off JONESY.

MICKEY: Any punishments will come from me.

RICHARD: I left him in your care.

MICKEY: He just ran off.

RICHARD: Why?

MICKEY: I don't have to explain nothin to you.

JONESY: My brain is dancing like the bees.

MICKEY: You've put us bang on top again now Jonesy.

JONESY: I have to follow the patterns.

MICKEY: They'll all be on their mobile phones to the pigs.

JONESY: Bees remember through patterns.

MICKEY: We have to go now.

JONESY: Bee memory and car language times yellow, equals
missing memory.

MICKEY: You've proper brought us on top now.

JONESY: Yellow car... Yellow something... Yellow something!

JONESY stamps his feet in frustration.

MICKEY: Ay, no tantrums.

JONESY: Yellow, yellow, yellow...beetroot!

JONESY pounds the table.

MICKEY: I won't tell yer again lad.

JONESY goes and stands in the corner, rocking.

MICKEY: I need to know what's goin on out there. Have you
got a radio?

RICHARD: I doubt it still works.

MICKEY: Where is it?

MICKEY starts trying to open the wall doors but none will open.

What's the fuckin knack with these doors?

RICHARD opens one of the wall doors and pulls out a radio and shoves it in MICKEY's hands. He then guides JONESY to the table and sits him down.

JONESY: The traffic is like the biggest fruit machine ever Richard.

RICHARD: Is it?

JONESY: Each lane, or road or avenue is like a roll in the fruit machine, and the yellow cars are like the bars. And once I can see the total pattern, then it'll come.

RICHARD: What will?

JONESY: The jackpot.

RICHARD: Try and relax.

JONESY rocks in the chair.

SIAN: Mickey.

MICKEY has been fiddling with the radio. It suddenly bursts into static.

MICKEY: Bingo!

JONESY: B.I.N.G.O. B.I. / N.G

MICKEY: Quiet! (*To RICHARD.*) What band's the local news on?

RICHARD: 1010 AM.

MICKEY moves the dial to the number but gets nothing but static, he tries moving it elsewhere but nothing, he continues to search.

JONESY: All this thinking is making me hungry.

SIAN: You can have this.

SIAN offers her bowl to JONESY.

RICHARD: You should eat it.

SIAN: I'm not hungry.

RICHARD: You need to get your strength up.

SIAN: He can have it.

JONESY takes the bowl.

JONESY: Before we got here you was like a neat nag.

SIAN: A what?

JONESY: A gannet.

SIAN: Red sky at beach.

JONESY: Pardon?

SIAN: That's an anagram for cheeky bastard.

SIAN, RICHARD and JONESY laugh.

JONESY: You got me there Sian.

RICHARD: How long have you been working on that one?

SIAN: Months.

JONESY goes over to the window to look at the cars. MICKEY keeps twisting but he just gets more static.

JONESY: Richard, it's snowing.

RICHARD goes over to the window, as MICKEY keeps twisting the dial.

RICHARD: So it is.

SIAN: I want to hold the snow Mickey.

MICKEY looks at SIAN.

MICKEY: What?

SIAN: It's snowing.

MICKEY: In the middle of May?

MICKEY looks over to the window. He looks shocked when he sees the snow.

MICKEY: Dead weird.

JONESY: Snowflakes are like honeycomb cells. They all have six sides.

RICHARD: Have you ever seen any under the microscope?

JONESY: No.

RICHARD: They're incredible. Every crystal is a masterpiece of design and no one design is ever repeated. When a snowflake melts, that design is lost forever.

SIAN: I want to touch some.

MICKEY tosses the radio.

MICKEY: It's fucked.

SIAN: Jonesy, will you go and get me some snow.

JONESY: Okey doke.

JONESY runs out. SIAN stands at the window and MICKEY joins her, as they watch the snowfall. RICHARD heads over to a cupboard and opens it. He takes out a musical instrument and starts to play a beautiful lamenting tune.

SIAN: God, they played this tune at my fifteenth birthday party. My dad asked me to dance with him and I told him no. He looked so hurt. (*Beat.*) Will you dance with me Mickey?

MICKEY: I can't dance.

MICKEY is unsure what to do.

SIAN: Come on I'll show you how.

MICKEY and SIAN start to dance together. Holding each other. They slowly spin around the room. JONESY comes back in holding two big balls of snow. As MICKEY and SIAN dance he sprinkles it over them. SIAN closes her eyes to take in the sensation. RICHARD comes to the end of the song.

Remember when it snowed last winter? It was so heavy. Jonesy lost all our money and I thought we were going to freeze to death. But you built an igloo Mickey and we all cuddled up inside it and do you know? I don't think I'd ever been so warm.

MICKEY: Me neither.

SIAN: I don't want to lose you Mickey.

MICKEY: Yer not gonna.

SIAN: But we want different things.

MICKEY: We need to get out of here.

SIAN: I want us to stay here.

MICKEY: We can't stay here.

SIAN: It's the safest place for you Mickey. They'll soon find yer out there. They'll take you away from me.

MICKEY: No, I know what I'm doin; I'll always be one step ahead. Look we need to make a move before we're snowed in.

SIAN: Can we stay here Richard?

RICHARD: If that's what you want.

MICKEY: Hang on a minute.

RICHARD: You will be safe here.

MICKEY: No thanks. Trust me, get in the car.

JONESY: I want to stay.

MICKEY: You don't know what yer want.

SIAN: I want us all to stay.

MICKEY: They're closin in on us now.

RICHARD: No one's coming here Mickey.

MICKEY: How do you know?

RICHARD: No one comes here.

MICKEY: We did.

RICHARD: There's no need to run anymore Mickey.

SIAN: He's right.

RICHARD: You can raise your child here.

JONESY: And keep bees.

MICKEY: Why would you let us stay?

RICHARD: Why not?

MICKEY: I don't get it.

SIAN: What's to get?

MICKEY: It's not right.

SIAN: What isn't?

MICKEY: What's in it for him?

RICHARD: I'm trying to help you here Mickey.

MICKEY: People don't help people like us.

RICHARD: You could be happy here.

MICKEY: I'm happy as I am.

RICHARD: I doubt that.

MICKEY: What do you know about it?

RICHARD: There will be no need to look over your shoulder anymore.

SIAN: He wants to help us.

MICKEY: We're nearly there now Sian. Next stop Blackpool and then it's Vegas and then our own place. Not his place. Ours.

JONESY: I don't want to go to Vegas Mickey.

MICKEY: I know what's best for us.

RICHARD: Look, it's up to you. You can make your own minds up.

SIAN: Then I'm staying.

JONESY: I want to stay Mickey, and keep bees with Richard.

MICKEY: Are you all livin in some sort of dream world or somethin? This isn't some magical island we've washed up on. And he ain't some fuckin wizard, who's goin to save us all from the shit we're in. Fuckin keep bees? I tell yer where yer wanna keep them, in yer fuckin heads, cos you've all got plenty of room in there.

RICHARD: You need to face up to the facts Mickey.

MICKEY: What facts?

SIAN: I'm sick of the life Mickey. I want to stop.

MICKEY: Don't say that.

SIAN: I know I pushed myself on you but there's a baby in here now. (*Strokes her belly.*) When I feel her move inside me, I feel so much love for her. And I want her to be safe. I want her wrapped up warm in a nice wicker cot, at the end of a warm familiar bed. I want you and Richard to build a porch swing, so that we can sit with her on warm summer nights and look at the stars.

MICKEY: We can have all that in Vegas.

SIAN: Now who's dreaming?

MICKEY: Look, I know best about these things. We're not safe here, so we're leavin.

SIAN: We're not.

MICKEY: I'll carry yer to the car if I have to.

RICHARD: Just because you've got some sort of desire to be a human tumbleweed, doesn't mean they do.

MICKEY: Don't get all smart with me.

SIAN: Relax Mickey.

MICKEY: I know what you're up to.

RICHARD: I'm offering you stability; a home.

MICKEY: And who are you all of a sudden, eh? Doctor Barnardo?

RICHARD: What are you so afraid of Mickey?

MICKEY: I'm not afraid of nothin.

RICHARD: You're afraid of forgiveness.

MICKEY: Forgiveness?

RICHARD: For not stopping your dog.

MICKEY: What have yer been telling him?

RICHARD: Well I forgive you Mickey.

MICKEY: Who are you to forgive me?

RICHARD: The outraged citizen.

MICKEY: You're off yer trolley you.

RICHARD: I've forgiven you; now you have to forgive yourself.

MICKEY: You two go and get in the car right now.

SIAN: No.

MICKEY: I'm not playin games.

SIAN: We can have everything we want right here.

MICKEY: I'm goin.

SIAN: If that's what yer want.

JONESY: Bye Mickey.

MICKEY paces the room. He's getting desperate. Losing it.

MICKEY: Don't do this to me. I've looked after yer haven't I? Looked after you and him?

SIAN: Yeah you have.

MICKEY: Yer can't just leave me on me own.

SIAN: You'll find someone else.

MICKEY: You have to come with me. (*MICKEY swallows hard.*) I love yer both.

SIAN is taken aback.

SIAN: Then stay here with us.

MICKEY: Jonesy?

JONESY looks at SIAN.

JONESY: I think I'll give up sugar now Mickey.

MICKEY's world collapses.

MICKEY: (*Turning on RICHARD.*) You've done this.

RICHARD: I haven't done anything.

SIAN: Leave him alone Mickey.

MICKEY: I don't know how you've done it but you've gotten into their heads somehow.

SIAN: He hasn't.

MICKEY: You've turned them against me.

RICHARD: You're paranoid.

MICKEY: Poisoned them.

RICHARD: You've done the poisoning. The minute you came across Sebastian, you should have taken him to the police. You should have at the very least stopped running and given him a home. And you should have left Sian where she was. But what do you do? You impregnate her and you hold him back.

MICKEY: What do you know?

RICHARD: You're a bad influence.

MICKEY: And what kind of influence are you supposed to be? Yer really think Jonesy's goin to be better off in your care?

RICHARD: He can reach his potential here.

MICKEY: He does good with me. He makes money. He has a friend. He's learnin how to survive. Do yer really think social services would have done him any good? They'd have put him back in with a couple of wankers, who'd have got rid of him as soon as he turned eighteen.

RICHARD: He'll be well looked after here.

MICKEY: Tell them they can't stay.

RICHARD: No.

MICKEY: I said, tell them they can't stay.

RICHARD: I feel sorry for you Mickey.

MICKEY: You feel sorry for me?

RICHARD: You're nothing but a lost monster.

MICKEY: And what do you think you are with yer little box of tricks?

RICHARD: There are no tricks here Mickey.

MICKEY: So who do yer think yer are then? God?

RICHARD: Would that be so hard to believe?

MICKEY lunges for RICHARD and grabs him round the throat.

JONESY: Get off him!

MICKEY: Think yer smart you?

SIAN: Don't Mickey.

MICKEY: Think yer fuckin clever?

RICHARD: Get off me!

JONESY picks up the candlestick.

You're strangling me.

MICKEY: Is that what I'm doin?

SIAN: Let him go.

MICKEY: I'm so thick I don't know what I'm fuckin doin.

SIAN: Mickey!

MICKEY: Yer a fake.

JONESY threatens MICKEY with the candlestick.

JONESY: Let him go.

SIAN: What are yer doin Jonesy?

MICKEY: Put that down.

RICHARD: Do as he says Sebastian.

JONESY: Not until he lets you go.

MICKEY: I said, put that down.

SIAN: Stop it!

JONESY: If yer don't let him go, I'm going to hit you with it Mickey.

MICKEY: Put it down!

JONESY: I'll count to three.

SIAN: Don't be stupid Jonesy.

MICKEY: Put it down!!!

SIAN tries to reach JONESY but she is too weak.

JONESY: I don't want to hit you Mickey.

SIAN: Both of you just stop it.

JONESY: One…

MICKEY: I don't fuckin believe this.

JONESY: Two…

MICKEY: I'll give yer one more chance to put it down.

JONESY: Three!

MICKEY: You want this?

MICKEY throws RICHARD toward JONESY, he lands at his feet.

RICHARD: (*Spluttering.*) Put it down Sebastian.

SIAN: Look at yer! Yer no better than a dog!

MICKEY: You'd have hit me?

JONESY: Yes Mickey.

MICKEY lunges at JONESY but JONESY strikes MICKEY hard across the head. MICKEY stumbles back; stunned as blood trickles down his temple.

MICKEY: (*To RICHARD.*) Yer know when I found him he was about to be raped by a bunch of big boys. He was all alone, must have been about seven stone. I knocked them into the middle of next week. Broke one of me golden rules. Put meself on top, made enemies and that ain't no good on the streets.

RICHARD: And that makes him your property?

MICKEY: Shut up! I took him under me wing and I protected him and give him a life. You've seen the money he's made.

MICKEY takes out the money.

RICHARD: He's worth more than that.

MICKEY: And then you get into his head.

MICKEY moves toward RICHARD. JONESY raises the candlestick.

JONESY: Don't touch him.

MICKEY: (*To JONESY.*) You're breakin my fuckin heart Jonesy. I took you on and now yer goin to throw me over for him? After all I've done for yer? I've kept it real Jonesy. No dreams. No false hopes. And you spend a few minutes with this fuckin prick. Who fills yer fuckin head with all kinds of shite. Gonna do this for yer and gonna do that for yer. Fix yer fuckin calculator. Turn yer life around; keep fuckin bees, get yer on *Mastermind.* You really think that twat's gonna do any of it? That piece of shit, who can't even face the real world?

JONESY: Yes.

MICKEY: Come on then. Get started. That last one only tickled. Take that and put everythin you've got into it Jonesy. Make sure yer don't hold back.

SIAN: Just go Mickey.

RICHARD: Don't do anything silly Sebastian.

MICKEY: No, come on, he's the big man now. You just make sure yer cave me skull in good and proper because you'll only get the one chance. Come on. What are yer waiting for? Do it! Do it!! Do it!!!

JONESY swings the candlestick and MICKEY blocks it with his left arm. The arm breaks and it falls to his side.

You've broke me arm.

JONESY strikes again, catching MICKEY across the temple. MICKEY staggers.

I fuckin love you.

JONESY strikes MICKEY across the head again and this time MICKEY goes down. SIAN screams. He manages to get up onto his knees. JONESY stands over him and raises the candlestick and is about to strike again...

RICHARD: No Sebastian!

JONESY hesitates. MICKEY takes the opportunity and side sweeps JONESY's legs bringing him down. Then MICKEY is on top of him and starts pummelling his face with blows with his good arm.

MICKEY: I fuckin love yer, yer little / bastard.

SIAN: / Stop it!

MICKEY: After everythin I've done / for yer.

SIAN: / Leave him alone!

MICKEY: He needs teachin.

SIAN: Is that how you're goin to teach our baby?

MICKEY stops.

RICHARD: There we have it. The epitome of man. Why did I think you'd be any different?

RICHARD starts restacking his tins.

MICKEY: I'd never hurt our baby Sian.

SIAN: I've put everything at risk for you.

MICKEY: I don't understand.

SIAN: Look.

SIAN puts her hands down her knickers and pulls it back out to show MICKEY the blood. MICKEY gets up.

MICKEY: What's that?

SIAN: I don't know Mickey but I should be showing it to a doctor in a nice warm hospital. Instead I'm hiding here to protect you and what do you go and do? (*Beat.*) I put you first, instead of my baby. I mean, I thought I owed you that much but I was wrong. I thought I knew you Mickey. I knew you were violent. You've had to be to survive. But I honestly thought you would never do that to one of us. You are a monster. I've risked everything for you but I don't even know who you are.

MICKEY: No, no, no. We just… We have to… I didn't know. We have to get to hospital. Get in the car.

SIAN: Your arm's broken.

MICKEY: I can…we'll just… Jonesy can change the gears.

SIAN: He's in no state to do that now.

MICKEY: Richard. Drive us to the hozzy. Richard.

RICHARD ignores them and continues to stack.

We have to get to hospital.

SIAN: And then?

MICKEY: Everything will be alright.

SIAN: Will it Mickey? And once the baby's born, you'll let them clean her up and then you'll bundle her in your coat and take her out onto the streets, so she can get used to her new home.

MICKEY: It won't be for long, just until we can buy our ranch.

SIAN: You really believe you're going to do that? (*Beat.*) How are yer going to make the money without Jonesy?

MICKEY: I need yer Sian. You and the baby.

SIAN: Jonesy needed you. He needed you to let him go, and now look at him.

MICKEY doesn't look.

Look at him.

MICKEY looks at JONESY. His face is covered in blood.

SIAN: He put his trust in you and that's how you repay him.

MICKEY goes over to JONESY who hasn't moved since his beating. He crouches down beside him and touches the blood on his face.

MICKEY: Jonesy... I'm... I'm so sorry... I... I didn't mean to hurt yer... I just... It's because...because yer mean so much to me... It's not about the fruit machines...honest...yer like me son.

JONESY doesn't move. MICKEY shakes him; nothing.

Jonesy?

MICKEY shakes him again. JONESY doesn't respond.

He's not breathin.

MICKEY breathes into JONESY's mouth.

Come on.

MICKEY does it again.

Breathe.

Still nothing. MICKEY pushes his stomach and then breathes for him again. Still nothing.

Please Jonesy.

MICKEY tries again. JONESY suddenly gasps and sits upright.

JONESY: There it is, there it is, there it is...yellow car...yellow car...yellow car... No! Yellow cot! Brown bed...blue covers...can't sleep... Mum and Dad's bedroom door is locked...need a cuddle...need someone...anyone... open Ellie's door...yellow cot...yellow covers...no baby sounds...glow worm...mobile of yellow ducks...climb in...cuddle up close...she's all cold...skin like fish meat... she's so cold... I'll keep her warm...maybe she'll come back then...hold her close...hair smells like roses...yellow roses...her closer...fall asleep...wake up... Mum is screaming... Dad pulls me out of the yellow cot...things start to come loose in my brain...shaking me... What

have you done?...shakes me harder... You've killed
her...buttons coming loose... Killed her, killed her...
Murderer...blacking out...nothing...nothing... Wake
up you little bastard... Is that an angry face or a happy
face...nothing... He didn't even cry... He didn't even
– tssssssss...nothing...beetroot...memory malfunction...
found it...pushed it to the back...behind the buttons...
I didn't kill her Dad...she was already dead... I just...
just wanted to make her better... Is that why you left me
behind? You all wanted to be with Ellie? You thought she'd
be afraid of me? Because I'd smothered her? But I didn't...
I couldn't tell you because you shook the memory to the
back of my head... Things came loose... I can see...see
them...buttons...buttons I never knew I had... This one...
this one will make me cry... I want to cry... I want to cry
for Ellie... I want to cry for Dad and Mum and Angela and
Antony and the baby and Mickey... I just have to press it.

*JONESY slowly moves a pointed finger to his forehead and presses
it and then lowers his hand. Nothing happens for a moment and
MICKEY and SIAN look at him. Then tears appear in JONESY's
eyes, and spill out and down his cheeks. He starts to sob and this
gets heavier, until he is bawling. RICHARD has stopped stacking the
cans and now goes over to JONESY. He puts his hand on his shoulder.
JONESY stops crying and smiles.*

RICHARD: Thank you Sebastian. You've finally taken control.

RICHARD removes his clothes as he speaks.

I thought I knew it all. I thought it was all finished. That
every drop of magic in the world had shrivelled and
evaporated under the glare of high definition television sets
and bright bleached smiles. I was convinced that all the
wonder had been replaced by logic and science.

*RICHARD opens a cupboard and removes a suit and, as he speaks,
starts to put it on.*

I felt that mankind was locked into the final route, heading
toward its inevitable end. Like you, Sebastian. A boy
totally disconnected from the bigger picture. Cut off from

nature, from magic, from empathy. Trapped by your brain into a route dictated by logic, just like humanity. But I was wrong, you just found a new pathway; your brain rerouted. The river will always find the ocean.

RICHARD is now dressed in the suit.

RICHARD: (*To JONESY.*) Do you think you can help Sian into the car?

JONESY: Yes.

MICKEY: What are yer gonna do?

RICHARD: I'll drive us to the hospital.

MICKEY: (*To SIAN.*) Then what?

SIAN: I'm going to have our baby and then I want to go home. And then I'm going to love her.

JONESY: Me too.

MICKEY and SIAN smile at each other.

Mickey, I forgive you Mickey.

SIAN: Me too.

The house groans. It is a sorrowful, pining sound. They look at the ceiling.

(*To MICKEY.*) I need some space. You can come and find us when the time's right. Come on Jonesy.

JONESY takes hold of SIAN and walks her out of the room.

RICHARD: (*To MICKEY.*) That baby needs you. You may not fit into that world Mickey but something tells me you'll make it work.

The house groans again.

We're going to change things Mickey. Put some magic back into the world.

RICHARD opens a cupboard and pulls out a big can of petrol. He starts pouring it around the room, backing toward the door. MICKEY waits for him there. RICHARD holds out his hand and MICKEY puts his lighter into it. The house groans again, louder than before, pleading, frightened. RICHARD ignites the lighter. Blackout.

THE END.

Printed in the USA
CPSIA information can be obtained
at www.ICGtesting.com
LVHW020847171024
794056LV00002B/433